Looking *after* yourself

A Christian guide to a balanced life

Len Kofler MHM

Director of the Institute of St Anselm, Kent

redemptorist
publications

Published by **Redemptorist Publications**
Alphonsus House, Chawton, Hampshire, GU34 3HQ UK
Tel. +44 (0)1420 88222, Fax. +44 (0)1420 88805
email rp@rpbooks.co.uk, www.rpbooks.co.uk
A Registered Charity limited by guarantee.
Registered in England 3261721.

Layout and cover design by Peena Lad

ISBN 978-0-85231-381-7

A CIP catalogue record for this book is available from the British Library

Printed by Nuffield Press, Abingdon OX14 1RL

Author's Note

This book is based largely on experience. You will find in it theory, guidelines and exercises for working on your own body, mind and spirit, and also a certain amount of autobiography, to which I sometimes turn for examples. Although it is intended as a personal guide to growth, it is not exactly a self-help book. It is based on the belief that when we grow as individuals, we assist society to advance as well. We are all interconnected. Our model for a fully human life is Jesus, and the book attempts to engage the reader with him during a journey towards greater freedom and fulfilment.

Looking after yourself is not primarily a theological or scholarly work, but I trust that it draws responsibly on an abundance of learning, ancient and modern. I hope you will find it of practical use, and that it leads to healing for you and the community to which you belong.

Contents

Chapter three Learning to affirm ourselves and others

Chapter four Getting to know our personal history and integrating it into our lives

Chapter five Learning to live a healthy life

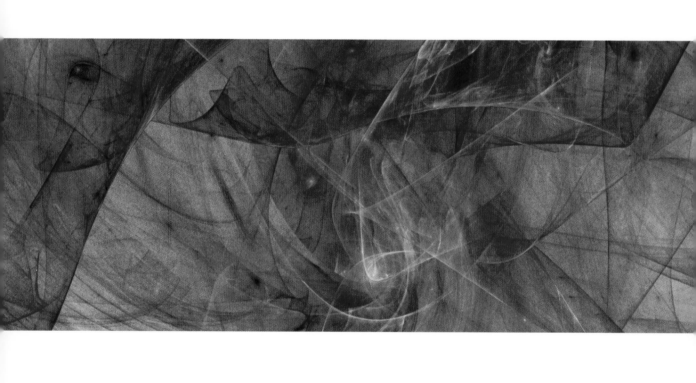

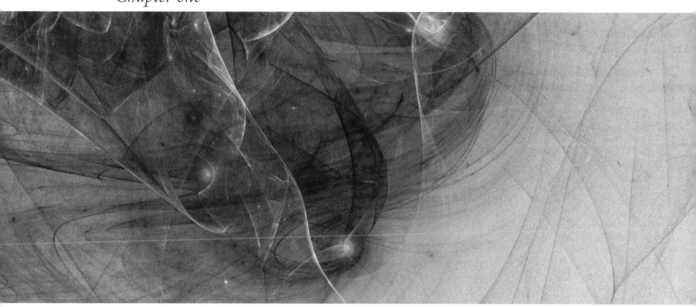

Chapter one

Learning to listen

The importance of listening

We listen all the time: we listen to the children, to our parents, to the radio, to the TV. We listen to the preacher, the teacher and friends. We listen to the boss and we listen to the customers. In fact we spend most of our time listening. But do we really listen? As we listen, aren't we often thinking about what we are going to say when it is our turn to speak? We hear what is being said, but fail to give it our full attention. Our mind wanders; we remember something we should do or should have done. Because we are not paying attention the speaker becomes frustrated and tries harder to make us respond, making his or her point more strongly. The listener resents this ear-bashing and thinks even harder about what to say when given the chance.

In today's world there is a constant bombardment of noise and distraction. We filter out most noise that comes our way, but in doing this we lose the skill of giving our full attention to others. Therefore, if we really listen to people, this experience will be exciting for them; they will open up to us and probably become our friends. Listening is so important because so few people feel listened to. When people are not listened to they try other ways of getting attention: children shout and make a lot of noise or become mischievous; adults may get drunk – and make a lot of noise. In extreme cases, discontented citizens may rouse others to march, demonstrate or riot.

When people are properly listened to, they feel they matter; they feel responsible and consequently act responsibly. Most of us have been entangled at some stage in red tape, and constrained by bureaucratic dictatorship. Here, listening is replaced by endless paperwork and complete subservience to a system, whether it functions well or not. If officials were permitted to really listen to those on the ground, they might get ideas of how to sort out problems effectively, not just on paper.

We may never have realised how important it is to listen. All we want to do is express ourselves, but perhaps we are afraid to say what we want to say. We may be shy about speaking up. Indeed, we may have struggled with this all our lives. For that reason we may have been quiet and said very little or even nothing. Being quiet and saying nothing is not the same as listening. Listening is a forgotten skill, but it is the most important skill we can learn. When people don't listen, mistakes are made.

Effective listening can help in professional and personal growth. It can increase productivity because employees feel appreciated. Good listening can help us sort out problems which we may have with one another. When people feel that they are important because they are listened to, they are willing to cooperate. By good listening we can arrive at fair decisions, prevent conflicts and improve the quality of communication.

Obstacles to good listening

Society is inclined to equate speaking with mastery and power. We use talking to gain political power or to sell a product or an idea; to persuade, and for verbal attacks; to relax during meals. We punish someone by refusing to talk or listen to them. Constant chatter has produced a cultural resistance to listening, while modern technology can impair relationships and communication. The mobile phone has many advantages, but it can also be extremely invasive. Listening itself, in the guise of headphones on the street, can become a barrier to the more human needs of listening, and can isolate the wearer from the surrounding environment. Where it is cynically observed, careful listening is often associated with weakness and apathy. Yes, it will take time, energy and awareness to learn to listen effectively.

A biased listener tends to distort messages. Often listeners get so emotionally involved that they are no longer able to listen effectively. "Red Flag" words can evoke strong feelings and can create obstacles to good listening. Sometimes we react to a word or phrase that has been conditioned by past experiences. This causes us internal disturbance. People resent it when they believe they are being judged and labelled negatively, and as a consequence often cooperate reluctantly. Tone of voice can be equally destructive. Frequently, for instance, a statement, which in itself is harmless, is taken as a slight because of the speaker's tone of voice. Family feuds can begin like that.

Positive words can affect us in a similar fashion. Let's call them "Green Flag" words. These can produce an emotional response that will interfere with good listening. For example, imagine yourself listening to a person who praises you for things you have done. Then she goes on giving you instructions about how to implement certain procedures. You could be so taken up by the positive remarks that you don't hear the procedures she wants you to implement.

So whether they affect us positively or negatively, the meaning we attach to certain words can affect our ability to listen. We filter words through our varied beliefs, knowledge, education, upbringing and experience in general. As a result, no two people attach exactly the same meaning to a word. People argue because they do not hear or understand words in the same way.

At certain times of the day we have more energy than at others, so tiredness plays a part in listening. When we are too tired we find it difficult to listen and be attentive. When we have problems, our energy is often used up dealing with them. We do not have enough energy left to use for good listening. The fatigue obstacle often intrudes during evening meetings; people may have used up a lot of energy during the day and find it difficult to listen. When we are not well this has an impact too.

There are also external distractions that make listening difficult. The speaker may be using insufficient volume, or talking in a monotone or unfamiliar accent, or talking too fast or too slowly. There could be loud noises such as traffic, machinery or seagulls. The room may be too hot or too cold. Frequently, phone calls interrupt the listening process. You may find yourself distracted by what is going on outside the window.

These and many more barriers make listening difficult. We have to practise becoming good listeners. We learn to listen by doing it.

Try it yourself

♦ Recall words or sounds to which you react strongly, whether positively or negatively. When did you hear those words or sounds for the first time? Try to bring the events back to your consciousness as vividly as possible. What connections do you discover between the words and your feelings? Think of some contexts in which the words or sounds could be used that might change their meaning.

♦ Reflect on the following list of factors that may affect your ability to listen: cultural differences; religious differences; social differences; tiredness; stress; illness; pain. Sometimes your own problems may be too similar to those described by your companion; sometimes they may be so different that listener and speaker find difficulty in understanding one another.

♦ Think about the ways in which your listening habits may be weak. Are any of the following typical of the way you listen?

★ I pretend to listen to people while I am really thinking of other things.

★ When the person's manner of speaking annoys me, I stop listening.

★ When people use certain words that I find offensive, I stop listening.

★ When the speaker uses difficult language, I switch off.
★ When a person talks in a monotone, I stop listening.
★ I stop listening when a speaker says things I don't find interesting.
★ When I think I know what the speaker is going to say, I stop listening.
★ When I am hurt or angry, I stop listening.
★ When a number of people talk at the same time, I stop listening.

♦ Think about the ways in which your listening habits are strong. Are any of the following typical of the way you listen?

★ I can easily follow what people are sharing.
★ When I listen to people, it energises me.
★ I feel great empathy for anyone to whom I am listening.
★ When people cry, I am with them in their sadness.
★ When people are cheerful, I enjoy it.
★ When people are angry with me or with others, I understand them.
★ When people are silent after they have said something, I wait before I respond, in case they want to share more.
★ I always try to communicate with people out of love.

What exactly is listening?

What is it not? It is not thinking what to say. It is not being anxious about expressing what we ourselves want to express. Neither is it feeling shy and failing to say what we would like to say. When we listen, we empty ourselves of all these preoccupations. We are interiorly still, and take in what comes from within or without. We are fully present to these things.

Listening is the perception of sounds with our ears. This is the most obvious sense of listening. But there are many sounds about us that we do not perceive. We do not often respond to the ticking of a clock, for instance, to the singing of birds in a tree or to the voices of passers-by. If we live in a noisy place, it is good that we do not listen to the noise.

What is true of the registering of external sounds is also true of our mind. Our mental world is bombarded with the internal "sounds" of thoughts, feelings, intuition and imagination. We do not respond to most of them. We have learnt to select the sounds that we respond to. We can learn to hear and perceive more by listening to these sounds. Poets, theologians, artists and mystics often listen to realities that are beyond our immediate sense experience. When we pray, we can listen to the highest reality.

When we listen, we take in information from ourselves, from others who speak, from the environment and from God, while remaining empathic, present, non-judgemental, open and emptied. We encourage the speaker to continue to communicate with us. We reply to the speaker by moving his or her ideas one step forward.

Good listening is a creative act. Often it is assumed that the speaker is more important than the listener, but the listener has the opportunity to create real communication by the way he or she listens. Often the listener tunes the speaker out, assuming he or she has grasped the gist of the message, and then, while the speaker continues, prepares a response, which might be quite inadequate. It may help us to become aware of our non-creative listening ways. A good listener responds to the content of what is being said, acknowledges the feelings expressed, shows understanding and encourages further sharing.

Try it yourself

Write down some of the poor listening habits you have noticed in others. Have you exhibited any of those habits? If so, write these down, with descriptions of how they have affected the situations or your experience.

Listening to the environment

Imagine a thrush sitting on the branch of a tree. This sight takes up your full attention. It is still and quiet and does not move. You are still and quiet and do not move. You are absorbed in the activity of watching and listening. You hear it utter a few notes. You see how the bird stretches out its head from time to time. You see how it turns its head in different directions and all of a sudden it flies away, and the sound of its wings makes a surprising impact. You have been attentive to this bird. For a minute or two nothing distracted you. While you listened, you were attentive and focused.

Listening to ourselves

We can gain self-awareness through listening to ourselves. People are often shocked when they become aware how frequently they talk to themselves. Their negative self-talk has become a habit. This negative dialogue can cause non-productive behaviours. This can be one way we lose our power. Such negative self-talk can consist of comments like "I am no good"; "I can't do that"; "I am incompetent"; "I am not beautiful"; "Nobody likes me"; "I can't communicate".

Listening to ourselves helps us to become aware of our feelings, beliefs, values, attitudes and behaviour. In the light of this awareness, we can begin to change what we want to change. This self-examination makes it possible to identify when thought processes are fruitful and when they are self-defeating. We can re-examine the beliefs that cause particular negative thought processes, and we can modify these beliefs. This will help us to be in charge of ourselves. Many beliefs were learnt in childhood and they have greatly influenced our life and our behaviour; they influence the way in which we talk to ourselves now.

As long as we remain unaware of these subconscious influences, we set up roadblocks to personal and professional development. These roadblocks result in non-productive behaviour, inner conflict, feelings of frustration and defeat.

Try it yourself

1. Think of a belief you have about yourself.
2. Examine how this belief influences your self-image.
3. In response to this belief and your self-image, what kind of things do you say to yourself?
4. Reflect how all this influences your attitudes and expectations.
5. In the light of this self-examination, what do you want to change?

Negative affirmations

These are often expressed internally. Negative beliefs lead to negative attitudes. We may believe that we can't listen effectively. This negative belief could lead to negative, internal affirmations, such as "I can't understand"; "I can't pay attention"; "I always lose track of what people say".

Our beliefs about ourselves affect how we talk to others. When we talk about ourselves, we confirm how we see ourselves and how we feel about ourselves. Listening to the way we affirm ourselves to others can help us towards changing old habits and perceptions of self. What language do I use to label my behaviour? Negative labelling leads to negative behaviour. By replacing the negative language with positive ideas we create self-respect and success.

Listening to our anger and expressing it constructively

People often repress their anger, and that makes it difficult to carry on a normal relationship. This is how marital relationships often break down; after years of cold war, and with no help from outside, a couple can't stand each other and get a divorce.

Anger that is not expressed in words will always find another way to express itself. Often it comes out in subtle ways. How? It finds expression in remarks which we make such as put-downs; insensitivities to our friends who have hurt us; forgetting things like birthdays and appointments; not fulfilling expectations. All this may be unconscious, but all these actions interfere with healthy relationships. If we can listen to our anger and express it in a constructive way without hurting others, we can probably deepen our relationships and grow more confident by gaining insights which will help us to mature.

Listening to each other

When two people listen to each other, they learn to understand each other; they learn to appreciate each other. They get enriched in this process. They become aware that they are different in the way they think, in the way they react to things, in the way they perceive things.

The differences between two people can lead to quarrels, conflicts, hurts and misunderstandings. However, if the two people really listen to one another, the differences can become sources of learning and mutual enrichment. Differences are often the cause of deterioration of relationships in families and in working situations; listening can turn them into a treasure. Parents who listen to their adolescent children can learn to understand young people in spite of the generation gap. If adolescents listen to their parents, they can save themselves from many blunders because they can learn from the experience of their parents.

Professions such as law, medicine and politics have an inbuilt demand for good listening. Take doctors, for instance: some doctors are good listeners. This makes them more capable of helping their patients, from whom they constantly learn. Some are not such careful listeners, which can lead to inaccurate diagnoses or the wrong medication being prescribed. Sometimes doctors are prevented from listening properly to a patient because of insufficient time being allocated.

When a doctor listens carefully, he or she discovers much about the patient's physical and psychological make-up. A patient who feels listened to and understood perceives that something has already been accomplished; listening is healing in itself. Many people were never listened to when they were children, and have a lasting need for somebody to listen to them.

Guidelines for good listening when talking to one or two people

♦ Be open, focused and attentive. We can create a positive attitude through nonverbal behaviour.

♦ Show interest in the speaker, his or her needs, feelings, values, areas of interest, hopes and expectations. Encourage the speaker.

♦ Do not be judgemental. "You are okay and I am okay." Be a mirror, a sounding board. Invite the speaker to bounce ideas and feelings off you. Reflect back what you think the other person is feeling or saying to you. This helps the speaker to be clear.

♦ Try not to ask too many questions. Questions can come across as an interrogation, and interrogations often trigger negative feelings.

♦ Don't let the other person hook you emotionally. This can happen when you get angry, hurt or upset, and can mean you allow yourself to get involved in an argument or jump to conclusions. Try not to pass judgement.

♦ Use different ways of indicating that you are listening, such as brief expressions: "Uh-huh"; "I see"; "Right." Also use nonverbal acknowledgement such as a nod, facial expressions (matching what the talker is saying); maintain a body expression that is relaxed and open; use eye contact and, occasionally, touch. Use invitations such as "Tell me about that"; "I'd like to hear what you are thinking"; "Let's discuss that."

Listening in order to help others

In the caring and helping professions, listening is of paramount importance. Most people were not listened to as children and, if they are in hospital or a nursing home, people often urgently need to be listened to. One often hears the phrase, "But you don't listen to me." Listening by itself can be very healing. When I was a young priest in New Zealand, my parish priest asked me to visit a husband and wife who were fairly recently married at the age of fifty and were finding their relationship difficult. I went to see them and listened. That was all really. I don't remember saying much or offering words of wisdom. At Christmas I received a letter telling me how I had helped them in their relationship.

Listening as a manager

Very often you hear the complaint that staff are not listened to. People don't know what is happening; they are confused; they feel they are not being taken seriously. Employees know more than managers often think. They have a lot more to offer.

A boss who listens earns respect and loyalty, and gains important information about how the business is going. A boss who listens to suggestions and complaints creates a healthy atmosphere in which employees like to work. An employer who listens encourages employees to grow and develop their careers, and when real listening occurs in the workplace, more is accomplished.

Try it yourself: an exercise for managers

Primary questions:

♦ As a manager, do I ever listen attentively to my employees?
♦ Do I see it as my main job just to give orders to people?
♦ Do I really listen to myself, to the environment, to others and to God?
♦ Where is my focus when listening to someone in my charge?

Secondary questions:

♦ Do I ever really listen to myself while I am talking or listen to those in my charge? What are my thoughts, my desires, my intentions? What is important for me? What am I feeling? Write down the answers that have occurred to you.

> *Repeat this exercise several times during the week. It is most important that we become aware of our inner life. Managers, like everyone else, can be helped by getting to know their inner world. The set-up of our inner life influences our relationships with other people.*

◆ Do I listen to the environment? What happens when I go for a walk? Am I so absorbed in my thoughts and worries that I ignore the beautiful sea, trees, flowers, cornfields? Or am I so involved in talking to somebody that I see nothing of the scenery? Write down your observations.

> *Repeat this exercise several times during the week. It is a great enrichment to have a healthy relationship with nature. It can have a tremendous healing effect on us. It can help us to rejuvenate ourselves.*

◆ Do I listen to those I manage or am I absorbed in my own thoughts, plans and problems? Sit down with a colleague and listen to him or her for five minutes very actively and without judging what is said. Later, write down what you experienced.

> *Repeat this exercise several times during the week. Active listening will improve your relationships with people.*

◆ Do I listen to God? Have I got time? Am I aware that my relationship with God is my most fundamental relationship which can inspire all other relationships, including with people I manage?

Learning to listen to God

God is the basic reality. Without God there would be no world. God is the great Living Reality and God's presence is within us and all around us. Listening to God can happen at prayer; the prayer of listening is a simple way to perceive that reality. The next step is for us to respond to what we hear. If we do not respond, at least within ourselves, we don't really hear.

Finding time to get to know God is also useful. Perhaps we could set aside time to pray every day, spending time alone with our God on a very regular basis. A sense of the presence of God becomes more and more difficult to recover once it is lost. That is the reason why it can help to spend a good deal of time with God regularly. People of all religions have prayed in the morning and evening; they begin and end the day by being conscious of God, their Father and Creator. If we persevere and seek, it will be given to us. If we keep on listening to God, things will be revealed to us.

We can learn to listen to God with mind and heart. To pray "with mind and heart" is a most valuable human experience: to learn to respond to all currents of life prayerfully; to listen to joy and to sorrow, to love and to hate, to peace and to anger; to learn to respond prayerfully to injustice, sin, death, crime, betrayal and whatever comes our way.

We can listen to God's word contained in the sacred books. For this we need the help of the Holy Spirit. Scripture helps us to change our mindset. It reminds us that without grace we do not have the energy or the inclination to listen to God. We need to desire to listen to God and allow God to influence us and teach us the way of life that leads us back to God. Desire enlivens the will with the expectation of delight. When we have learnt to delight in reading sacred scripture, we will be filled with a desire for it. If we listen to the sacred books with attention, desire and delight, then the printed words become precious and valuable to us.

Even if we are very familiar with the Gospels, we may feel we want to fit them into our present situation. We could ask, "What will I hear from the Lord in this reading to sustain me in the day ahead?" We could find passages which apply to our life situation and which give us spiritual food for the ups

and downs of daily life. Just as we need physical food, we also need spiritual food, and each person's diet varies. Our convictions are important; they are a sign of a deep faith. Whatever we do in this world has great importance for our life in the world to come. Christ in his life has shown us the way to his Father. We are invited to go the same way. Therefore, we profit a lot if we put ourselves into the shoes of Christ as we meditate on his life and teaching. He is the model for us. Let this model speak to us. Let us carefully listen to him and his words. What does all this mean to us individually?

To read the scriptures is to hear the word of God. Therefore, we read scripture with reverence, attention and prayer. We read within the context of the tradition of the Church and remembering the historical background of the writings, so that we do not arrive at a merely private interpretation of the scriptures. Purely academic approaches to scripture often do not nourish the spiritual life. If we read the Bible with attention, desire and reverence, our hearts start burning within us as it reveals deeper meaning for our own lives.

As we listen to the word of God in the liturgy of the Mass with a great desire to be enriched by it, we begin to appreciate the seven sacraments. We can find constant food and enlightenment by the impact of the words. In the sacrament of reconciliation we hear the words: "And I absolve you from your sins, in the name of the Father and the Son and the Holy Spirit." These words are like honey for a guilt-ridden soul.

An essential aspect of our spiritual life is to learn to respond to the gifts of grace that come to us every day. They come in so many different forms to us: a friend, a book, an illness, a shock, a disaster, a joyous event like the birth of a child and even a funeral. Life events provide us with many opportunities for prayer. Through prayer all these events become graces, great opportunities for us to grow and come closer to Christ.

We can help ourselves by listening to the reality of life and stripping ourselves of our preconceived expectations. To do this we need the virtue of hope. Hope is the grace to believe that whatever happens to us, God will provide us with the necessary ingredients of salvation. Once we have found out the message of life we must try to integrate it with our efforts to live by the Gospel. Slowly we see things in a new light.

God has told us that we should not be greedy. God has told us that there is more to life than just accumulating money, prestige and power. Listening more closely to God can help us all be more faithful stewards of our material wealth.

Listening to nonverbal communication

Much of what we communicate is not verbalised. It appears in our body language. Even when a person is not talking, he or she is still behaving in a certain manner. Listening to nonverbal messages is one of the most important skills we need. People convey much through facial expressions: face colour changes as people talk about things they have strong feelings about; movements of the lips, mouth, cheek muscles and eyebrows can give us information about what is going on in the person we are listening to. We can learn to pick up messages through nonverbal communication that indicate tension, doubt, trust, inattention, joy, depression and so on. People are often unaware of their own nonverbal behaviour.

The tone of voice is an important factor in finding out more about the feelings of the person talking to us. These feelings are often not expressed verbally. The nonverbal communication is mainly unconscious and therefore less likely to be manipulated or disguised by the person. We might get a truer picture of what the person is feeling by picking up these messages than we would get from their verbal communication. The skilled listener hears more than just the words of the speaker. He or she listens to the pitch, rate, subtle variations that the tone of voice is indicating.

Nonverbal communication makes it more difficult to hide what we feel. For example, I once said to a student, "You seem to be angry with me." She replied: "I am not angry!" Her face was flushed; she clenched her fists; her lips were trembling. Often people create a façade by successfully choosing words. However, they are fooling themselves. They may think they have covered up their emotions, but unconsciously the emotion is being expressed tonally or through gestures. Some people try to camouflage anger with smiles, but tone and body language will probably give them away. You will notice that shrugged shoulders are often used to convey indifference, when the issue being discussed is important. A quivering lip may indicate an effort to prevent crying. A person who avoids eye contact may indicate dislike, lack of interest or embarrassment. These nonverbal factors are clues to help us figure out what is going on between us and the other person.

We need to keep in mind that we tend to interpret what we hear and see through our own internal filtering of experience. Sometimes painful past experiences are generalised to other, similar situations. This is what is technically known as "transference". The present experience triggers the memory of the previous situation. This in turn influences the person to interpret the other's behaviour through a highly charged filter. Because of this, communication can break down.

Practical Revision

How can I make listening a beneficial experience?

♦ Avoid being critical, argumentative and judgemental.

♦ Listen to the speaker's underlying meaning; don't allow your mind to wander.

♦ The timing for asking questions is very important. It is usually best to hold your questions until you have listened carefully.

♦ Abstain from solving the talker's problem or doing the talker's thinking for them.

♦ Make eye contact but at the same time do not stare at your companion.

♦ Watch for their posture and gestures. Unconscious body language can reveal the truth if there is a discrepancy between words and gestures.

♦ Don't allow your own feelings or distractions to disturb what is being said.

♦ Be patient, because the time and attention you give may be precious.

♦ As you listen, get to know the personality, likes and dislikes, motivations, ambitions and values of the speaker. This will help you to respond.

- Be aware of your own prejudices and how they interfere with your listening.
- Use words and phrases to indicate that you understand and want to encourage the person to keep on speaking: "Of course"; "I know what you mean"; "I see". Nod or smile where appropriate. Do not sit back and absorb passively.

What are the attributes of a good listener?
- Keeping an open, curious mind;
- Listening carefully, so as to understand properly;
- Being self-aware and listening to others with the whole self;
- Becoming personally involved with what is said;
- Not necessarily responding conventionally to what is said;
- Listening to the essence of things;
- Remaining mentally alert.

Conclusions

To sum up, here are some ground rules. Avoid the following: interrupting the speaker; rehearsing in your own head what to reply; interrogation or teaching. Avoid giving advice; rather, reflect back to the speaker what you observe and how you believe the speaker feels. (You can always ask for clarification when you are not sure what the speaker has said.) A good listener makes friends easily; people flock to people who listen to them. A good listener will learn many things all the time, even when talking to children. A good listener will be an instrument of healing, and will repair the deficit of a lack of listening in childhood. A good listener is a great facilitator of communication, and will help shy people to come out of their shell. Careful listening is an authentic expression of love. People feel appreciated when somebody listens to them, and a good listener is a great gift to others. Ultimately, no kind of listening is more important than the attention we pay to what God is saying to us.

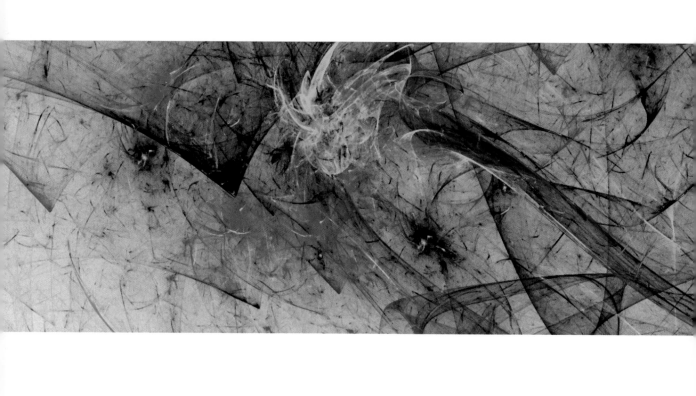

Chapter two

Becoming more aware...

...of ourselves

As we grow in our ability to listen effectively, and as we listen particularly to ourselves, we become more aware of what is going on inside. We will slowly discover what we are feeling at any given moment and we will discover the thought processes that may trigger some of those feelings. We will become more aware of our behaviours and discover the way we communicate with and relate to ourselves and others.

Many people go on a long journey to see what other countries are like; others love to discover nature. Some want to discover the animal world; others the world of plants. There are people who are very interested in minerals; they visit many countries, gathering their collection. Yet there remains this other journey. Are you interested in discovering what is going on inside yourself? Becoming aware of our inner world is an exciting journey.

If we are not aware of what is going on in our body, mind and spirit, we cannot bring about any change that might be very beneficial to our well-being. We may not even realise in what our well-being consists. Many people think that they are on the right track, provided they have plenty of money; they think that plenty of money will make them happy. Others may think that provided they have good physical health, they are perfectly happy. However, there are people who have plenty of money and good physical health and are still not happy; they do not feel fulfilled. They do not experience life as meaningful. They are looking outside, rather than inside. Becoming aware of what is going on inside ourselves may help us to find meaning in life, to feel happy and fulfilled.

…of our bodies

Many of us are not aware, or are only partly aware, of what is going on in our bodies. But we become aware of our body when one part of it aches. For example, we are aware when we have a headache, stomach ache or back ache but often have no idea what the message is that the ache is transmitting. We don't know how this pain originates in our body.

Some of us are totally alienated from our bodies. Others spend hours and hours looking after their bodies, while at the same time neglecting other aspects of their being. It is so difficult for us to get the right balance. We are body, mind and spirit, but most people do not spend enough time caring for all three in an integrated fashion. We may not see any link between our daily problems and coping with tension. We may not be aware how body, mind and spirit are interconnected and interrelated. We have separated if not dissociated them. We are no longer aware of the unity of our being.

In my book *Healing Relationships* I have described in detail how I see the human being and the human personality. I try to demonstrate that we need to become more aware of what is going on in our bodies and observe in which physical areas we experience tension and emotions. The body is just as much a part of us as the mind and the spirit. When we neglect any one of these dimensions of being human, we damage ourselves.

There are people who have basic problems with their bodies. They can't accept that they are small or tall, fat or thin, black or white. Some years ago, I knew a woman who rejected herself and had a very poor self-concept, because she thought her nose was too big. At school other children had given her the nickname "big nose". As she kept psychologically and spiritually working, and slowly learnt to accept that her nose was an integral part of her, her whole self-worth improved. She became a very outgoing person. Before that she had been extremely shy and reserved.

Some people cannot accept their gender. This is particularly true in certain cultures; I have known several Indian ladies who wished that they were male. Often I found in my counselling sessions with them that their parents had expected and wanted a boy. So when they were born, their parents found it difficult to accept them as girls, some of whom were brought up as though they were boys. Consequently, they identified strongly with the male gender role. These girls picked up the message that there was something wrong with them. All of them seemed to be much happier once they had worked through this gender issue.

When I give a talk about mid-life crisis, I say it does not matter whether you feel as male or female. Whatever characteristics you acquired in the first half of life need to be complemented by the opposite gender characteristics. What we have not developed in the first half of life, we need to develop in the second half. We will only feel fulfilled if we are in the process of developing those aspects of our personality that have not so far been developed.

There are people who struggle with accepting their sexual organs. During therapy sessions I often find out that such people had been told as children, or somehow picked up the idea that these organs are "bad". Consequently, they are almost bound to feel bad about themselves. They might go so far as to feel that they are "bad people". They don't know why. Slowly, as they discover where this comes from, they are able to learn to accept their sexual organs and themselves. This is a gradual process, because the false notion of guilt is often deeply embedded in the unconscious.

Try it yourself

♦ When you have a few minutes, sit quietly and observe what is going on in your body. Do I experience tension in any part of my body? In my shoulders? In my stomach? In my legs? In my hands? In my head? In my neck? In my back? How is my breathing? Is it shallow? Is it fast? Is it slow? How do I hold my body? Is it bent over or upright?

  Repeat this exercise several times during the week. Slowly you will become more aware of your body experiences.

♦ Have a nice warm bath and observe how you feel in your body. Go through the whole body and see which part is relaxed and which is tense.

♦ Can I accept that I am male or female? Do I accept the size of my body?

♦ Do I feel my sexual organs are "bad"?

...of our thoughts

What is going on in my mind? Am I bombarded with many thoughts? Are they contradictory? Are my thoughts positive or negative? Books have been written on positive thinking. Very often our thoughts are not positive; in fact they can be very negative. They can do us much harm without us realising it. As we discover our negative thoughts, we can change them to positive thoughts. For example, if we say to ourselves, "I am no good" which is a very negative thought, we can change it to: "There are things I am good at and there are other things I am not so good at." Nobody is good at everything. We all have our limitations. Equally, everybody has areas in which they are successful.

As we learn to listen to ourselves, we become aware that an inner conversation is going on in our minds. We may discover two different voices within. Sometimes they may support each other, at other times they will be in conflict with each other. One is the parent inside us and the other is the child. When they are in conflict with one another, a problem arises. These two voices go back to the earliest years of our lives; one is the child which we were when we were small, the other relays the parental messages which we picked up when we were young. Both of them may be very active in us now as adults. The more we learn to be aware of, and distinguish, these two voices, the more we will be able to bring harmony into our lives by listening to both of them and by trying to find a solution to the conflicts going on within us.

Let us look at our inner child. Often this inner voice deals with needs or activities of the here-and-now. It may cry: "I am hungry"; "I am tired"; "I am bored"; "I want a hug". This voice can be insistent and demanding.

A great strength of the positive inner child is its enthusiasm and curiosity. Children want to explore new territories. The positive inner child loves to have fun: it loves playing games, it is keen to learn new things, it practises new skills. The inner child has a deep desire to please the parents. The inner child is in charge of the emotions and the energies. The inner child records all the impressions it receives through the five senses.

We also need to look carefully at the negative inner child. Many children are neglected and abused. They experience negative emotional programming. Thus their eager-to-please attitude is replaced by resistant and rebellious behaviour. The negative inner child can have stored irrational ideas in its memory. These can be the result of severe trauma. Such traumas might be the death of a loved one, an accident or a separation as through divorce.

These traumatic effects are still with the inner child and need healing. If not healed, they can cause addictive or compulsive behaviours. Among these are chemical dependencies, excessive dieting or food bingeing. People with these tendencies can be unhappy and may not experience the joys of life.

Let us now look at the voice of the inner parent. This voice reflects the programming received from our parents or parent substitutes. We start to develop our parent voice at a very early age. Our inner parent takes on many characteristics of our outer parents' personality. If we had much contact with our grandparents, they too will have contributed to our inner parent. Teachers, priests, television personalities and peers may have made their contribution to the inner parent voice within us. Even social and cultural factors may have had their influence.

In adulthood the inner parent uses the stored-up memories of our programming, partly positive and partly negative. Let us look at the positive inner parent. It can be a good teacher, giving us healthy advice and guidance. It can be a soothing voice that is ready to help and support the inner child. In fact it can nurture the inner child when it is in need of it. It can calm the inner scared and angry child. In fact, it can provide whatever the inner child needs. It can provide stability for the inner child. It can help in the making of rational decisions.

Let us also look at the negative inner parent. It can be quick to judge and to lecture the inner child. It can make major life decisions without the consultation of the inner child. It can be overly critical and even threatening. It can overpower the inner child so that the inner child loses its joy and enthusiasm. So both will suffer. The negative inner parent can ignore the needs and desires of the inner child.

Try it yourself

1. Find a quiet space and start a dialogue between your inner parent and your inner child. Do it as if they were two different people. Let the inner parent start the conversation: "Dear inner child, I am your parent. I would like to get to know you better. That is why I would like to talk to you for the next twenty minutes. I would like that the two of us understand and enjoy each other. For this to be achieved, we need to spend time together on a regular basis. I will ask you questions; feel free to answer them. I will also listen to you and try to understand you. Sometimes I will make mistakes and may become judgemental. I don't intend to hurt you. I apologise now for any mistakes that I might make. Let us work together and support each other."

2. As you get involved in the conversation, do not be surprised if the answers are not the ones the parent expected. This may be a sign that the inner child is talking to you. Write down the answers of the inner child. Use the exact words that the child uses. Accept the answers of the inner child. Thank the inner child for its responses. At the end of the session express your joy for the conversation you had. Express also your gratitude to the inner child for cooperating with you. And fix another time when you will have another conversation.

3. Keep a record of your conversations and date them. Each record contains your inner parent's questions and the answers of your inner child.

4. As things progress, the parent can vary the questions he or she puts to the inner child. Here is a list of possible questions. Allow the parent to choose those that are applicable to the situation. "How are you feeling physically today?"; "What emotions are you experiencing right now?"; "What is your favourite kind of music?"; "What do you think about your childhood?"; "Did you like going to school?"; "Who were your best friends at school?"; "Did you enjoy your birthday parties?"; "Do you feel comfortable during these sessions?"; "What would make you feel more comfortable during these sessions?"; "How did you sleep last night?"; "Do you remember any dreams you had last night?"; "Whom do you love most in the world?"; "What was the happiest time in your life? Tell me about that time"; "Can you remember a time when you were enthusiastic and full of energy? What made you so enthusiastic and energetic?"; "Can you think of a time you felt afraid?"; "Can you think of something you wanted but did not get? How did you feel about that?"

These are some examples of questions the inner parent can put to the inner child. Obviously, the inner parent will pursue the theme in a natural, conversational way, leading the inner child and being led by the inner child. At the end of each session, it is recommended that the parent asks the following question: "Is there anything else you would like to ask me or tell me before we end this session?" This gives the inner child a chance to share or ask something important.

As you pursue these inner conversations, the inner child and the inner parent get to know each other much better. They can begin to cooperate with each other and sort out any conflict that may arise.

...of our emotions

One of the most important areas for increasing awareness is that of emotion. Many people do not know what they are feeling most of the time, so they can't use or properly control their emotions. Often, they are captives of their emotions, so that they react to situations in ways that they later regret. Being aware of our emotions gives us the possibility of learning to use them constructively. A further step is to learn to choose our emotions. Many people are afraid of emotions, particularly anger, so they learn to repress it. They may have learnt as children that anger was bad or sinful, so they tried never to get angry.

However, anger always finds an expression, even if it is in unconscious ways. Some of these expressions may affect the body in the form of psychosomatic illnesses like stomach ulcers, headaches or heart problems. Other expressions of repressed anger show themselves in covertly aggressive behaviour known by therapists as passive-aggressive behaviour. This is unconscious and interferes with the well-being of another person. It is an indirect way of expressing anger. It may be in the form of sarcasm, subtle putdown statements, being late, forgetting things or avoiding people.

The more we become aware of the emotion of anger, the more we can use it for our own or for another person's benefit. Very often anger has a message for us, which may well be that we are being confronted by danger. The emotion of anger can help us to deal with this danger. For example, if somebody has been aggressive towards us, we can share our reaction with that person. He or she is quite likely to apologise and try to avoid this behaviour in the future. Your relationship will probably improve.

Many people have allowed themselves to be dominated by fear; they avoid many occasions where fear might be triggered. They may have rationalised this situation and told themselves that because they don't like certain things, they don't expose themselves to them. As they become aware of these fears, however, they can slowly start challenging themselves and, prudently, taking small steps, enter these situations and gain freedom from the apparent threat. Very often, we have to face the fear and do what we are afraid to do. Avoidance is not the solution to the problem of fear.

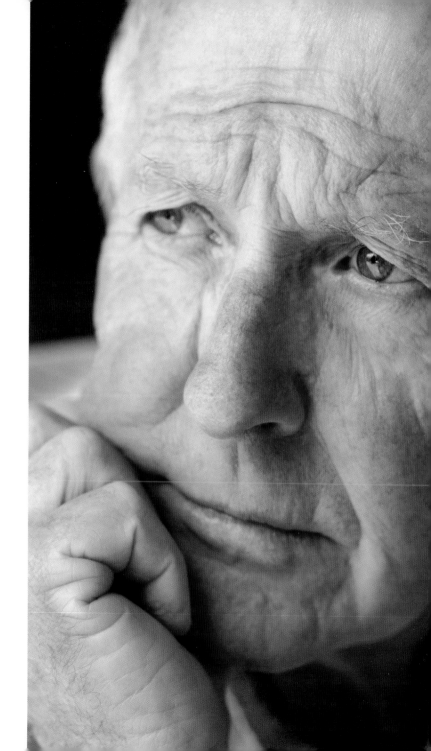

It may help us to know how we learnt to fear certain things. For example, when I was eight years old, I climbed a mountain with my brother, who was four years older than me. We had no equipment for climbing. When we were about two thousand feet up we could not climb any further because of an overhanging rock. We tried everything. We wanted to go back, but that would have been even more dangerous than climbing higher. In the end we decided that since I was too small to climb the rock, my brother would climb over it first, and then lie against the rock and pull me up. I was terrified, looking

down two thousand feet, while he pulled me up. Since then I have always had a fear of heights. Only recently have I noticed some improvement with regard to this fear, as a result of some supervised body work. It is amazing how long it can take.

For most of my life I have been afraid of dogs. When I was a small child my brother said to me, "Dogs bite you." From that day onwards I was afraid when they growled or barked or just opened their mouths. Sixty years later, a friend and colleague acquired a dog. At first I was afraid of it; I would not touch it. After a month or so, my friend said, "He knows you now, you can touch him." So I did, but only on his back, because I was still afraid that he would bite me. Slowly I could move my hands towards the dog's head. I watched how dogs played with each other. Although their mouths might be open, they are quite gentle with each other. Slowly, as I got used to the dog and observed and related to him, I got to like him. After some time, I started playing with him. I became more and more daring; I put my hand into his mouth! He would pull faces and I would pull faces. We had great fun with each other. After six years, the dog had to be put down. I really missed him. For me this had been a remarkable journey from fear to love. Love does cast out fear and fear casts out love. In order to grow in love, we have to deal with our fears.

Dealing with fears is a very complex matter. Sometimes it is good to become aware of the fears that may unconsciously interfere with our life. We may avoid getting married because we are afraid of the opposite sex. However, we rationalise it and say, "I am not meant for marriage" whereas the deeper truth is that we are afraid of the opposite sex. When we become aware of our fears, we can look at the history of the fear as mentioned above. Then we can also ask ourselves, "How far, if at all, have I learnt to cope with the fear? Is the way I cope with my fears healthy? Or do I need to desensitise them, by starting to relate to the object of the fear instead of avoiding it?" Sometimes avoiding it may be the best thing for us. It may not be so important for us to relate to the object of the fear. I saw my fear of heights in that way.

Some people are enslaved by their fears. There was the case of a woman I knew who was afraid that she might kill herself by taking pills. There seemed to be some connection with the fact that her father and her sister were both doctors. As she dealt with that fear, the object of the fear became a medal of Our Lady. They had many medals of Our Lady in the house. She was afraid that the medal would turn black and that would mean disaster for her. At another stage her fear was that she would kill children, so she was afraid even to pass a primary school. When the object of fear keeps changing like this, it is clear that the original and deeper fear has not been dealt with.

Other people have learnt to feel guilty about many things about which they do not need to feel guilty; they have learnt this habit in their families. As they become aware that some guilt-feelings are irrational and totally inappropriate to the situation, but understandable from their childhood experiences, they can challenge the thought processes that produce the guilt-feelings and replace them with updated ones. As children we all pick up messages from our earliest social environment that need correcting as we grow up.

If we constantly think we are no good, we will feel depressed, downcast, unappreciated, unloved and worthless. As we feel these emotions, we can ask ourselves what thoughts produce these feelings. Once we are aware of our negative thoughts, we can, sometimes with professional help, gradually change them to positive ones, which will have a lasting effect on our feelings.

Try it yourself

♦ How do I deal with my anger? Do I repress it? Do I shout when angry? Am I passive-aggressive? Do I hurt people with sarcastic remarks? How can I learn to deal with my anger more constructively? Are people afraid of me?

♦ What are some of my fears? How did I learn them? How do I cope with them? How can I grow in love by dealing with my fears? Which fears block me from growing in love? Do I avoid the object of my fears?

♦ Am I full of guilt-feelings? How did I learn them? Are my guilt-feelings rational or irrational, appropriate or inappropriate to the given situation? What further steps can I take to deal with my guilt-feelings?

♦ How aware am I of my feelings? Which steps do I need to take to become more emotionally literate? Am I aware of the advantages of becoming emotionally literate?

♦ What concepts about emotion shaped my behaviour in the past? Have my views changed?

♦ What difference would it make to my life if I were more in control of my emotions?

♦ Which emotions do I enjoy, and which do I dislike?

♦ Do I succeed sometimes in choosing my emotions?

♦ Do some emotions carry me away?

...of our behaviour

If we constantly feel negative and miserable, that will affect our behaviour. As children we learn all kinds of behaviour. I know a man who is very miserly. He used to secretly hoard money as a little boy. He is now a grown-up man with a family and he has still the same mentality. He wants to save money at any cost. Even if it is very cold, he won't put on the central heating; he goes on a holiday with his family and expects his sister to do the cooking for him to save money. With tremendous patience his sister has at last helped him to become aware that, for his own sake and that of everyone else, he needs to change this behaviour pattern.

For years and years I was not aware of how I was damaging my body by the way I stood and sat. Finally, I suffered from a slipped disk. Then I subscribed to a series of sessions in Alexander technique. I was made aware of my bad postural habits which I have since been trying to alter. It is a constant effort to maintain correct posture, but it is worthwhile doing so. My overall health is much better. In fact, it is better than it has been for many years.

Very often, people are not aware how they communicate with themselves and others. They learnt to communicate in a certain way as small children, perhaps sounding and looking aggressive, or assuming hostility where it does not exist, and still have the same behaviour patterns. This causes problems for themselves and others. A religious sister once asked me what I thought about liberation theologians. She had just read a book about them. I replied that I found some very good and others not so helpful. Her reply to this was an outburst of anger: "Why do you put me down?" I mirrored back her anger. She shouted at me with quivering lips, "I am not angry." We eventually worked through her angry reactions.

There is quite a large group of adults who had to learn at a young age to look after their younger siblings. They are now forty or fifty years old and still try to look after everybody they meet. In this way they get very tired. However, they don't know why they are so tired. If they become aware of this behaviour, they can change it.

Some workers have laboured hard all their lives and have exhausted themselves. However, they are not aware of this; it has become natural for them. By becoming aware of their damaging regime, they can change it and feel much happier.

Then there are the constant arguers. People avoid them, as they don't want to get involved in rows. They feel lonely. They are not aware of their behaviour because it is second nature to them. Becoming *aware* is extremely important for them so that they can change their destructive manners. Becoming aware is important for us all.

Changing behaviour takes time. We need to be patient with ourselves. Only repeated efforts will lead to success. There is no quick fix. When we persevere in changing our behaviour, we not only succeed in changing it, but also learn to be patient. It takes time to acquire a new habit, just as it took time to acquire the habit which we want to change.

Some people have learnt to say their prayers in a routine way. They find it no longer fulfilling and fruitful. However, since they are not aware that they could change the way they pray, they just carry on praying in the accustomed way. They are not aware of the possibility that they can change their manner of prayer to something more significant for them. For example, they could start a more meditative prayer life, saying their usual prayers, but in a slower, more meditative way.

...of how we communicate

If we are very negative towards ourselves in our thoughts, feelings and behaviours, we will communicate negatively with others and with God. Communication is an essential aspect of relationships. As children we learn incongruous methods of communication, partly as a result of realising how to get what we want. We may, for instance, have learnt to use many why-questions, and now people feel that they are being interrogated. We may have learnt not to look at people when we speak with them. Since we miss out all the non-verbal communication, this may often lead to misunderstandings. Once we become aware how inappropriate these habits of poor communication are for adult relationships, we can start to adjust.

Vocal communication is most important. Our voice may be very soft when we speak so people cannot understand what we are saying; we can learn to speak up. Conversely, our voice may be too strong, so people grow wary of us. Once we become aware of such vocal characteristics, we can gradually change them. As a result, it is probable that our relationships will improve.

Try it yourself

Some guidelines that may help you to improve communication:

- Communication needs to come out of love. Love is its basis. We communicate to build each other up. Any other motive will interfere with good communication. Good communication needs to be constructive. Some motives for good communication are to improve our relationships, to do away with misunderstandings, to encourage each other, to caringly confront each other; to share our joys and sorrows, our excitement, worries and stories with one another.

- In good communication people listen carefully and compassionately to each other.

- When we feel the need to talk to someone and that person has time to listen to us, we need to converse soon, because, if we leave it too long, we may never communicate what we wish to, and this could deprive both of us of possible growth. Or we may communicate in such a way that the other person does not get the message, because we no longer feel so strongly about the issue. Or we may come across too strongly, because we have ruminated too long over the issue.

- Good communication needs to be clear and precise, otherwise it may lead to misunderstandings. Writers and speakers often use flowery language and confuse others by doing so; some speakers go on rambling away and in the end the listener does not know what his or her point is. Others are not clear in their thinking and inevitably confuse the listener. It is important that we are clear in our mind about what we want to say.

- Effective communication needs to be as direct as possible. In some cultures people experience directness as threatening, and speak to each other mainly in indirect ways, but in a multicultural setting this could lead to serious misunderstanding. Indirectness can be hazardous because the person we are speaking to may not understand what we are saying, and may interpret it wrongly. Moreover, it is not wise to say something to a third person, hoping it will be passed on to the person with whom we really intend to communicate. This is dangerous, because the intermediary may distort the message we want to send. In this way we make ourselves very vulnerable.

♦ Reasoned communication tolerates disagreement, which in itself is often creative. Healthy disagreement can be creative and can help us to clarify issues. On the other hand, destructive criticism or disagreement is very often an expression of concealed aggression and as such is to be avoided.

If you answer "yes" to some of these questions, you need to work on these aspects of communication:

♦ Is my voice generally too soft or too commanding?
♦ Is my way of communication sometimes vague?
♦ Do I confuse people when I communicate with them?
♦ Do I go in for flowery language?
♦ Am I manipulative in my language?
♦ Do I tend to want to control people when I communicate with them?
♦ Are my motives for communication sometimes unclear, even to myself?
♦ Is my way of communicating aggressive?
♦ Do I have the impression that people don't listen to me when I speak?

If you answer "yes" to these two questions, you are already making progress:

♦ Do I try to express my love for people when I speak to them?
♦ Is my communication usually friendly?

So what would I like to change in the way I communicate?

...of how we relate to ourselves, to others, to the environment, to God

People often want to improve their families or communities but they don't know how to go about it. What can we do to improve our families, our communities and our parishes? Improving our personal relationships can help. We can do this by learning to deal with our emotions constructively and fostering healthy communication. These are the two central factors in improvement. It is not a quick fix. It requires hard work on the part of all those concerned. However, they need to know what to do.

Relationships are basic to our human condition. We depend on relationships when we come into the world. We learn to relate in our families and maintain these patterns as adults. What we experience in the first weeks after we come into this world, from our mother or mother substitute, becomes the basis of all relationships later in life. A child may quickly learn, because of unfortunate things that happen, that he or she can't trust people: mother, father, brothers, sisters or minders. Distrust will then be the basis for that baby in all relationships. Alternatively, the baby discovers that his or her parents and others are available, loving, caring, and they learn instinctively to trust them. This will create the basis for trusting people in general. Seeing that we learn these ways of relating in the first place, we can unlearn those that are not constructive, and replace them with more positive attitudes. This process should improve the quality of our life, and we should be much happier as a result. Of course, it is not simple; it needs a good deal of work and perseverance.

For example, if we become aware that we constantly put ourselves down during interior dialogue, we can choose to change that to a more positive way of communicating with ourselves. We may have learnt to hate or despise ourselves. As we become aware that in this way we are our own worst enemies, we can refuse to adopt that attitude, and learn to understand ourselves. We may discover many positive sides to ourselves, and then make interior communication more creative. Instead of constantly saying "I should" or "I ought to" do such-and-such, we can teach ourselves to say, "I want to do this", "I like to do this" or "I have decided not to do this." By using this language of choice, we begin to empower ourselves and feel much better for doing so.

If we become aware that our communication with others is very aggressive, we can change it to assertive. We will find that our relationships will improve, and friends will be more likely to want to be with us.

If we become aware that we are destructive towards the environment, we can learn to care for it, and derive great pleasure from doing so. In many ways we are wasteful with the resources of the earth. Slowly we are learning to be more careful. More and more we become aware how destructive we have been towards the environment, and very slowly we are learning to be more prudent and more concerned about mother earth. We still have a long way to go.

Finally, if we become aware that communication with God has become problematic, because it always tends to be negative, we can make a determined effort to change. For example, if we experienced our own fathers as strict and domineering, so that we were afraid of them, we may experience God in this way. Realising that God is different from our fathers, we may slowly challenge our fear and start to talk to God as a loving father or friend. Our whole relationship with God may change, and we may start to experience God as merciful, caring, understanding and loving.

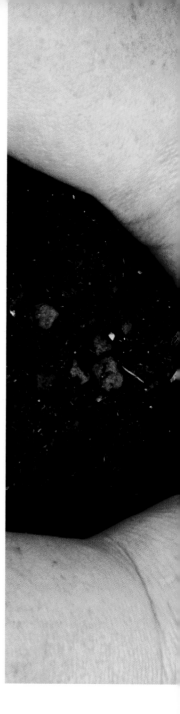

Try it yourself

Spend some time reflecting on each of the following questions; once you have completed your thought process about each one, write down the simplest and shortest answer with which you are satisfied.

♦ Do I love myself or hate myself?
♦ Am I very hard with myself?
♦ What aspects of myself do I not accept?
♦ What parts of myself do I appreciate?
♦ Am I aggressive in my behaviour with people?
♦ Do I love or hate people in general?
♦ What type of person do I dislike?
♦ What type of person do I find it easy to get on with?
♦ Am I really interested in other people?
♦ Do I go out of my way to assist others?
♦ Is the environment a profound concern for me?
♦ Is my life built around my belief in God?
♦ Do I want to deepen my relationship with God?
♦ How can I improve my relationship with God?
♦ Do I ever really thank God for all the good things he has given me?

Conclusions

Becoming aware of ourselves is the first step towards changing those aspects of ourselves which we wish to change. Self-awareness helps us to gain more control of ourselves, of our lives, our bodies, our thoughts, our feelings, our communication, our behaviours, our relationships. The quality of our lives will improve, and we have every hope of becoming happier people. Our lives become more meaningful and exciting. Every day can become a new challenge for us to grow as individual people in many ways, and to enrich our lives and those of other people. As we relate better to ourselves, to others, to the environment and to God, we feel more fulfilled. We experience ourselves as having a positive contribution to make to society and to the Church. We become aware that we are all interrelated and dependent on one another and called to help each other. We are the big family of God. We are in God's hands and care. This will provide us with a certain peace, tranquillity and hope. A whole new world opens up to us when we become aware of what is going on inside us and in our relationships with the external world.

Chapter three

Learning to affirm ourselves and others

It is important for us to learn to affirm ourselves when we perform well. Many people never affirm themselves. They are very hard with themselves. They put themselves down. They blame and belittle themselves. They focus on the negative aspects of their performance and life. This perpetuates low self-esteem which is the cause of many things that go wrong. If we do not believe in ourselves, it becomes a self-fulfilling prophesy and leads to negative outcomes on all levels. High self-esteem leads to positive outcomes. The question is: How can we affirm ourselves and others?

Being positive with ourselves and with others

We are aware how positive thinking affects our whole being and our achievements. A positive attitude to life energises us. People like to be around those who have a positive attitude, whereas a negative attitude paralyses us. People tend to avoid those who are pessimistic.

Being positive means seeing the good side of ourselves and others. It implies focusing on talents, abilities and strengths, rather than on weaknesses, limitations and shortcomings. It means being content and happy with what we have, rather than always wanting more and being dissatisfied.

A positive person will achieve more than a negative person because he or she has more energy and vitality. Enthusiastic people inspire others, because enthusiasm is contagious. A positive person will always see new doors opening. Being positive releases creativity; new possibilities move us forward and excite us to try them out.

Negativity, on the other hand, blinds us. It sees no future. It leads us to give up, even to despair, whereas optimism looks into the future, sees many possibilities, drives us to adventure.

When we are positive towards others, we see their beauty rather than their ugliness. This attitude releases energy both in us and in the other person. We allow the other person's talents to emerge, and we try to foster them. A commercial enterprise with positive people will be much more successful and effective than one which is suffused with negativity.

When parents see the good sides of their children, the children feel secure. When parents appreciate the diverse talents of their children, the children will be inspired to develop them. When a husband and wife appreciate each other's accomplishments, they create an atmosphere of security for the family.

Similarly, when a parish priest sees the positive sides of his parishioners and encourages them, such a parish will flourish. There is so much potential in each parish, but very often it does not get a chance because the parish priest does not see it or does not use it. Do seminaries teach future priests to be positive? Do they develop a positive attitude in their candidates?

When teachers see the positive sides of the children they teach, their overall performance improves. Schools need to have a positive approach and instil hope into the children as a preparation for their future life. Positive teachers can do any amount of good for children. Who helps teachers to become positive? Do they learn it in teacher training colleges?

How much happier a religious community is when the superior aims to discover the potential of each member of the community and allows it to flourish.

If a street gang were to discover the positive potential of its members, it could become a force for building up the environment rather than destroying it.

Respect for ourselves, for others, the environment, life and God

Respect is essential for living happily together in any organisation. It is in the family that we learn respect. Parents have a vital role to play in this process. Respect shows itself in the way they hold their children, the way they talk to them, the way they respect the place of each one in the family, the way they feed and dress them. All this can have a modelling effect.

When I walk through the streets and observe some parents, I am very much aware how they model the opposite of respect, when they shout at their children or hit them or drag them along to school.

I often feel inclined to address this with the parent, who most likely had a similar role model and can't help it, and thinks he or she is doing the right thing by getting the child to school in this way. I feel great empathy for both the child and parent and often wish that I could help them.

Every human being deserves respect, and primarily one needs to learn to respect oneself. Only once we respect ourselves can we respect others, the environment, life and God. Respect has become something of a rarity. Many citizens, I fear, have little concern about keeping roads, buses, trains or the environment clean. Some have no respect for each other. They push themselves forward, never mind how it affects others. They have little respect for themselves.

What does it mean to have respect for ourselves? It means that we keep our bodies clean and look after them. It involves dressing properly. It involves eating and drinking moderately and healthily. It also means setting aside time for ourselves. It means developing and using our potential. It means looking after mind, body and soul. We need to develop our intellectual faculties, and our spiritual lives. It is care for our whole being, not just for our body or soul or mind.

Since we are social beings, respect means establishing healthy relationships with other people. Healthy relationships involve clear boundaries. This means not intruding into other people's space. We have no respect for others if we dominate them, if we abuse them or exploit them in any way. We can abuse people by shouting at them, by avoiding them or ignoring them. If they need our help, we can support them. If they go astray, we can encourage them to come back. There are so many ways in which we can show our respect for other people.

Respect for an elderly person is shown when we greet them, when we vacate a seat for them, when we open the door of the car and close it for them. Some of these too have become rare. Years ago they were common practice.

Respect for life is a consequence of the fact that we are created by God. God is the Lord over life. Our job is to bring life to fruition on all levels. The physical life needs to be seen in connection with the spiritual life. When the physical life deteriorates, the spiritual life often grows stronger, because people have more time. Ultimately, we cannot judge whether life is still worth living or not. A doctor said to my family, when my brother was unconscious for seven weeks, "Let him go." We all prayed that he would come out of the coma, and he did.

Respect for oneself, others and God creates a certain positive atmosphere. We show respect for mother earth when we do not pollute it, when we look after it. My father was a farmer. He looked after the fields. He would make sure that the earth on steep slopes, when it came down, was put back where it had been. He would look after the forests, clean up fallen trees, cut down a tree where there were too many. His relationship with nature was a great example.

Both my parents had enormous respect for God. I could see it in the way they prayed, the way they received the sacraments, the way God was the centre of their lives. They could manage to cope with much suffering and hard work, because they saw it as an imitation of Christ in his suffering. Christ was at the centre of their lives. They would say the family rosary in the evening after hard work. This respect for God permeated their whole life. They showed enormous respect for their neighbours and also for strangers and poor people. They would give to those who were poor when they could hardly afford it. Deep down, they were very happy people with a family of nine children.

Try it yourself

- Where do we learn respect? How can parents model respect for their children?
- What does it mean to respect myself and others?
- What happens when we do not respect others?
- What is the basis of our respect for ourselves and others?
- What does having respect for life involve?
- How can we show respect for the environment?
- How do I express my respect for God?

Discovering our strengths and using them

We all have strengths, but sometimes we are not aware of them and therefore we cannot use them for our own or other people's benefit. Often we are not aware of our talents and we need another person to point them out to us.

It is so important for children to discover their strengths. It is good for children if their parents and teachers affirm them in their good performance and achievements. When they take time to support children by pointing out their strengths, children will soon discover their worth and their talents. Many people have low self-esteem because they never discovered the positive sides they have. They were always focused on what they could not do. As parents and teachers we have the great opportunity and responsibility to avoid this and to build up in children a healthy self-worth.

The earlier children discover their talents and strengths the surer they are to choose the right jobs and hobbies later in life. Children can easily become destructive because they want the attention of others and this is the only way they have learnt to achieve this. As parents and teachers we can forestall such destructive behaviour by teaching children to find constructive ways to get the attention they need. In this way life will be easier for children, parents and teachers.

The strengths we are talking about are very varied. You may be good at sport or you may be good with your hands. Some people have a very sharp intellect. Others use their emotions in constructive ways and are highly intuitive. Some people are exceptionally witty and humorous. Others are kind and understanding, and help wherever they can. Some people have a highly developed spirituality. Some people have a great capacity for love; they reach out towards others, they support them and encourage them; they listen to their stories. These are strengths that may reveal themselves at almost any stage in life. If they are not observed and encouraged, they may be lost or not fully used. What are the effects when children and people discover their strengths? They can learn to use them and so enrich the family, parish, school, society and Church.

Try it yourself

- ♦ Why is it good for us to discover our strengths early in life?
- ♦ When did you discover your strengths and talents? Are there still some that may be hidden away, of which you are dimly aware?
- ♦ Why do children become destructive?
- ♦ What role can a parish priest or teacher play in helping parishioners to discover their strengths? Have you profited from someone else's insight into your talents?

Write a brief essay in answer to this question: "How will society and Church profit if many more people become aware of their strengths and use them?"

Discovering our weaknesses and limitations and accepting them

We all have weaknesses and limitations that we need to learn to accept. It is a sign of maturity to accept one's limitations and weaknesses. Some people push themselves beyond their abilities and consequently suffer. We cannot be good at everything, so it can help to be satisfied with our strengths and accept that we have limitations. A mid-life crisis can be seen as a crisis of limitations. One challenge of a mid-life crisis is to learn finally to accept our limitations.

Often we may not be aware of our weaknesses because we have pushed them into the unconscious. There they wait to trap us later in life. What we cannot cope with in life, we repress. We need to bring our weaknesses out of the unconscious and integrate them into our conscious mind.

What are some of these weaknesses? We may be aggressive and repress it; but we can never succeed in fully repressing it. It will come out in indirect ways when we don't expect it. For example, we might repress our anger with the boss at work, because we are afraid of the repercussions of giving vent to it. We go home and find the meal is not yet ready and the children are noisy; we get irritated and shout at the children. Later on, we regret it. We realise that our anger and irritation were all out of proportion. Or we may never become aware how we transfer anger from one situation into another situation.

There are people who envy other people's fortunes, talents or achievements. They can't bear it if others do better than they do. They get terribly upset. Because this is too painful, they repress their envy, rather than face it. Other people are jealous in their relationships. They find it difficult when those close to them befriend others. This causes them a lot of pain. Some people want to earn a lot of money, but can't find a job with the kind of salary they want. They find this most difficult. Some want to go to university, but have not got the ability to do so and suffer enormously. Some children would like to be a famous football player, but only manage to stay in the local team. It is good to aspire for more than we have, provided that it is realistic and achievable.

We can only be happy if we learn to accept our limitations and weaknesses. As long as we repress them we are not dealing with them. Contentment is a virtue we all need. We can be happy with what we have and not strive beyond our capacities. Many people are very happy although they have very little. Many with severe limitations are very happy. And many who appear to have everything are unhappy.

Discovering the power within ourselves

It is easy to become frustrated when we feel powerless or dominated. Are we really powerless, though, or do we give power away? We may have learnt to give power away to others and need to learn to regain it. How often do we say, "I have to do this. I must do that. I should not have done this. I should have foreseen that. I cannot do this." This is all "slave language". Instead, we need to learn "master language" through which we empower ourselves: "I choose to do this"; "I like to do that"; "Next time I will make more effort to foresee things"; "I will learn from what I did." When we use slave language we give away power. When we use master language we regain it. We had to learn to give power away when we were children, and we still do it as adults.

As we learn to take responsibility for our lives we regain or gain our inner power. As long as we blame others for our misery, our misery will remain with us. As soon as we take responsibility for our misery, we can change at least some aspects of it. It is not easy to learn to take responsibility because then we have nobody to blame. We grow so used to blaming others. This brings us some satisfaction, but long term misery.

We need to become convinced that we are responsible for what we do. We can change many things. Only we can change ourselves. Nobody else can change us. As we become more loving, compassionate, caring, understanding and kind, many of our relationships will change. People will feel attracted to us. A power goes out from us that does something to other people. They may like to be with us. We may become their friends, whereas before they were afraid of us.

We are made in the image and likeness of God. God is love. So we are intrinsically loveable. This is the power within that we can discover and develop. As love flows out from us, love returns to us. It is in this love that our inner power resides. This power will grow, as our love grows. We are all called to emanate this love.

Try it yourself

♦ How and why do people give power away? Does this apply to you?
♦ Do you use "slave language"? What is the remedy?
♦ What happens to us when we blame others?
♦ How do we regain power that we have given away?
♦ What are the implications of being made in the image and likeness of God?
♦ What is the real power within me?

Developing a healthy playfulness

Playfulness energises us and makes life much easier; heaviness and sombreness can cripple us. Some people are too serious and make their lives unbearable. Some playfulness would help them to lighten the heavy burden they experience. Children are very playful. Unless we become like little children, we cannot enter the kingdom of God. Heaviness pulls us down, whereas fun and humour lift us up. Playfulness is linked with creativity. We need to allow the child within us to come out. Children dare to venture out and try to explore the world. They have a tremendous curiosity.

As we grow older, we may become too serious and cautious because of the negative experiences we have had. This can block us from going into the future with an adventurous mind. Obviously, we can also learn from the so-called failure experiences and turn them into learning experiences. However, let us still keep our playful and curious attitude, now enriched with the learning experiences.

Healthy playfulness can be part of our pastoral ministry, of politics, of economics, of teaching, therapy, social work and any other human activity. Often we are too stuck in the way we do things and lack creativity. This applies even to our prayer life. We may have got stuck in forms of prayer that no longer nourish us.

Flexibility, which is an aspect of playfulness, tends to be totally absent from public sector departments that decide how we should live. There is no time for anything that does not fit the bill. Too many laws and regulations kill creativity. State employees in charge of enacting legislation act only according to the programme they have learnt. If a new situation arises, they are lost. This is not their fault, but it means that those whom they are meant to serve are treated like infants and behave like robots. They may become incapable of living in a complex society and resort to doing stupid or dangerous things. We need creative minds that will do justice to the complexity. When we put everyone into the same pot, we do an injustice to the dignity of persons.

It looks as though too many people who make the rules have insufficient practical experience or independence to differentiate between different kinds of human situation, while those who are required to carry out the regulations obey them in a way that turns the human beings with whom they deal into a number.

Even our manner of play has become too serious. It has become inordinately competitive. The higher levels of sport have become for many a source of wealth. Games have become grindingly hard work. Unless you win, you are a failure. Where has playfulness gone in our play?

Try it yourself

- ♦ What is healthy playfulness? Do I possess it?
- ♦ What can we learn from healthy children about the nature of play?
- ♦ What happens to our playfulness as we get older? Can you sense this happening to you?
- ♦ What can we do with our failure experiences?
- ♦ What happens when governments introduce too many laws and regulations?
- ♦ Where has playfulness gone in play?
- ♦ Do I put too much emphasis on winning?
- ♦ Play a board game that you have not played for a long time.

Learning to love ourselves and others

The great command is to love yourself as you love your neighbour. It is a most difficult thing to learn to love oneself. Some people grow up hating themselves. They have become their worst enemy. They feel they are no good. They have heard this so often that they have got used to believing the negative voice within them.

Because many people have never received the necessary love from their parents, later in life they have to learn to re-parent themselves. In this way they can slowly learn to love themselves and others. This is a slow process. It is well worthwhile, however, since their quality of life will improve considerably.

The ability to love is a learnt thing. Usually children learn it in the family. It is learnt in loving relationships between husband and wife and between siblings. Love is expressed in many ways in a healthy family. The husband cares for his wife and children. He is sensitive to the needs of his wife, and she is considerate towards her husband. Both care for their children. They spend quality time with them. They affirm them. They play with them. They go for walks together. Together they go to church on Sunday and pray with their children. In doing these things they learn not only to love each other but also God. God becomes the centre of their lives. God gives meaning to their lives and particularly also to their suffering. An old proverb states, "The family that prays together stays together." This faith in God becomes more and more the basis for their family life and their values. Right at the heart of family life is love, which involves each member making sacrifices for the others. This has its own reward for children, the feeling that "I have done something good."

Children learn respect and love for their neighbours. Because they care for others, antisocial behaviour does not come into their lives. A society built on the principle of love does not need more and more police and prisons. A selfish and individualistic society does, because the government has to make sure that selfish individuals do not harrass their neighbours.

This shows us how important the family is for both state and Church. We also need loving priests and ministers who have learnt the lesson of love in their family of origin. If they have not learnt it in the family, it is useful for them to learn it during their years of training. The same holds true for teachers, social workers, politicians and business people. Love is the cement of society; it holds us together. Rules, laws, police and prisons cannot achieve that.

Our love needs to be based on the love God has for us. Religion is meant to play a cohesive function in society. When religion disappears, society breaks down. There is, of course, what we regard as the negative side of religion: fanaticism, intolerance, terrorism. But these are not true religion, they are aberrations of religion.

Try it yourself

♦ What is the great command?

♦ Why do some people hate themselves?

♦ How is it that some parents do not succeed in teaching children to love themselves and others? What would such parents need to do?

♦ How do parents teach their children to love themselves and others?

♦ How far is prayer linked with learning to love?

♦ How does modelling love by parents affect the children?

♦ According to your experience, how far is religion a cohesive force in society?

♦ "Love is the essence of our Christian religion". Prepare a talk for a debate on this statement.

Finding meaning in our lives

Life for many has become a struggle because they see no meaning in it. Day in and day out they have to get up in the morning and go to work. This too often becomes a burdensome routine. There is a meaning, though, and when we know it, it permeates all other meanings: God's purpose in creating humanity. He created us to share in his own life. He calls us to search for him, to get to know him, to love him. He calls us together into the unity of his family, the Church. The Church was founded by his Son Jesus Christ, our Redeemer and Saviour. He invites us in the Holy Spirit to become his adopted children and heirs of his life.

We are God's adopted children. This expresses our highest dignity as human beings. The Christian purpose in life, when fully expressed, is for a man or woman to work every day to become more like Christ, who came into this world to show us the way to his Father in heaven. Every day is a gift from God; every day is a great opportunity to work through some area in life that was wounded.

Daily encounters with others are great opportunities to show and express the meaning at the heart of our lives, and in that way to grow in love. Jesus showed his love for us by suffering and dying for us on the cross, although he was totally innocent. How could my day pass without suffering as a follower of Christ? With this attitude in mind, we might not be surprised when suffering turns up. Suffering needs to be met by faith in Christ, this is the Christian's greatest treasure. Jesus says: "Take up your cross and follow me." Suffering will always be with us. However, the thought that suffering can help us to grow and mature and become Christ-like, means that it is never meaningless.

Without meaning in life, it becomes unbearable. Some people despair because they cannot find any meaning for living. Others find meaning by increasing their wealth. Some people find meaning by supporting and helping others. For some people the meaning in their life is sport, for others it is entertainment. The deepest possible meaning, we believe, is to follow Christ and to make him our model.

Try it yourself

1. What is the meaning of life for you? Ask others this question, to discover what different answers there are.
2. What happens when people can find no meaning in their life?
3. What is the relationship between my suffering and Christ's suffering?
4. How can every day be meaningful and a challenge?
5. What does "Take up your cross and follow me" mean for you?

Learning to use crises as opportunities for growth

It is important for us to realise that crises are opportunities for growth. We all go through many crises in our lives. Each one is an opportunity for growth. A mid-life crisis particularly is an enormous opportunity for us to go deeper. The frustration we may experience at mid life may be a pointer that we need to change something. However, the change needed is not out there in changing a job or marrying another spouse, but in ourselves. It may imply a more radical way of living. We may need to focus on the essentials in our life. We may need to learn once more to pray and play. We may have neglected aspects of our personality and vision, such as tenderness, beauty, wonder, spirituality and so on. Instead of saying verbal prayers, we may find fulfilment in being quiet and reflective. Instead of doing things, we may need just to be. This is not easy for us if we have been constantly busy.

Many people when faced with crisis, particularly mid-life crisis, avoid all those painful feelings like frustration, disillusionment and disappointment and throw themselves into more work and more activity, instead of slowing down and becoming more reflective. Mid-life crisis invites us to go inwards, not outwards. It invites us to become like little children so that we can enter the kingdom of God. It means rediscovering our playfulness.

A crisis in marriage may mean that the two spouses need to spend more time with each other, so that they can rediscover the positive sides that they admired when they met in the first place. Through many steps of growing in love they will find that they will be able to establish a much deeper and more solid relationship than they had when they started out. Their communication will improve as they learn to listen to each other. They will become aware of many emotions in their life that they repressed as children and that are still interfering with their relationship. The husband may have had a hidden fear of women because of a very strict mother; now he becomes aware that it is not his wife he is afraid of, but his mother. He learns to live more in the here-and-now. The wife may have had a similar fear of her father, which she has transferred to her husband.

Priestly and religious crises are also opportunities for growth. Once the priest or religious finds the meaning of the crisis, it is possible to respond to it in a growth-producing way. The priest may have been very active and neglected his own spiritual life. Now the crisis invites him to develop a deeper spirituality that will lead him to fulfilment.

One thing is clear: discovering the value of love rather than of individualism is important. If we really love ourselves, we have no need for extravagant financial profits. We will be perfectly happy with less. We don't need to be greedy and accumulate wealth. Love for ourselves and others will prevent us from greed, because we want everybody to be happy and have the necessary means for living. That is at the heart of affirmation.

Try it yourself

♦ What is the link between crisis and growth?
♦ What is the meaning and grace of the crisis between husband and wife?
♦ How can a crisis help a married couple?
♦ What is the meaning and grace of the priestly crisis?
♦ What are the possible meanings of our recent global economic crisis?
♦ What do we need to do when we face a crisis?
♦ Is a crisis a positive or negative thing for me?

Conclusions

There are many ways in which we can affirm ourselves and others. As we have seen we can develop a positive approach to life in general. Respecting ourselves, others, the environment, life and God, is an act of affirmation. Discovering our strengths and using them for ourselves and others implies affirmation. When we learn to accept our weaknesses and limitations, we are involved in a process of self- and other-affirmation. Once we discover the power within ourselves, we will no longer be involved in power struggles. Healthy playfulness enhances self-esteem. As we grow in love for ourselves, and as we find meaning in our lives and learn from each crisis, we will find it easier to love others, and will find many ways to affirm them.

Chapter four

Getting to know our personal history and
integrating it into our lives

There is an old Greek proverb: "know thyself". Without self-knowledge we are very vulnerable. We don't know why we are doing what we are doing. We are not aware of our motives, our emotions, our values and many other things. We are probably driven to do things or rebel against doing things we are asked to do. It is likely that we do not make enlightened choices. The Greek proverb encourages us to make every effort to get to know ourselves, so that we can choose what will truly be best for us. One way to get to know ourselves is to discover more about our history and our unconscious material.

Exploring my personal history to understand myself better

Some people know very little about their personal history. They know very few basic facts. Others know many historical facts, but still do not know themselves. Do we know the history of our emotional reactions, of our transferences (those things that come from the past into the here-and-now), of our values, our sexuality, our drives, compulsions, inclinations, of the ways in which gender has affected our lives and of the development of our spirituality?

Since we are speaking of highly personal reflection here, it seems only reasonable that I should start with an example from my own life. When I was three years old, one of my aunts came to visit. We were in the sitting room. I noticed how my aunt favoured my oldest brother, John, by constantly pointing out how clever and good he was. I felt rejected and went to my bedroom. I decided that I would show her that I was as capable as John. I gradually and only half-consciously turned this rejection into a powerful drive to succeed in whatever I did. I became the bravest in the family; I was not afraid of darkness; I was not afraid of other boys even if they were older. I went to Mass every day. Education and higher education gave me plenty of opportunities to succeed. I became a priest, a missionary, a lecturer, and so on. I'm not saying that my perceived rejection by my aunt was the sole cause of all this, but I am quite certain that it was the original spur. I only discovered this source of my adult journey during an intensive workshop some fifty years later.

Here is another illustration of how we can acquire self-knowledge. A client, twenty-eight years old and with two degrees, came to me for counselling. His problem was depression. He was newly married, and he shared in the very first session that he was teaching Christian doctrine, but found it difficult to believe in a God whom he regarded as domineering. He was having great difficulties with the Principal of the college and also with his wife. He was somehow afraid of both of them.

As we explored his family background, it became clear that his mother was very domineering. In fact, in one session he reported that he had recently wanted to talk to his father on the phone, but his mother would not allow him to do so. He did not have the courage and energy to be assertive because, as we found out, he repressed his emotion of anger. One day he came to the session in an almost rapturous state: "I have experienced real anger for the first time in my life!" he exclaimed. Slowly he got in touch with his anger and the source of energy behind it. I encouraged him to phone home and ask to speak to his father; he succeeded and was very pleased with himself.

He became aware that he had been afraid of his mother because she was so strong and domineering, but he had learnt to repress his anger. He also became aware how he projected his fear of his mother onto his wife, the Principal of the college and onto God. After another five sessions his depression was gone. His problem with the Principal and God disappeared; his relationship with his wife improved.

However, that was not the end of his trials. Because of his hard work on himself he changed so much that he went through a terrible identity crisis. One day he came to the session with homework in which he refuted thirty-three assumptions he had built up in his life. That night he woke up and said to his wife: "Who are you? What are you doing here?" This frightened them both, but when they had spent time together answering these questions, they discovered they had the secret for a better future.

These two short case studies show us how our personal history, particularly in the family, can shape us. As we come to comprehend that personal history, we shall begin to understand ourselves better; this will free us from negative developments. The way we relate in the family will influence all our future relationships. Therefore, we need to know about it as clearly as possible. From this knowledge we start to understand why we behave the way we do. The awareness of this will help us to change what we want to change.

Obviously, we learn positive and negative things in our families. The positive aspects are our asset; the negative things are our burden. This burden can be changed. That is the beauty of being human. We can change, grow and become more integrated. What a fascinating and adventurous future there is for all of us, provided we work on ourselves, often with the help of somebody else.

So we confront the present moment with our personal history. Each time you find a person difficult to get on with, ask yourself, "What is it in me that makes me feel uncomfortable in the presence of this person? Is it their size, race or gender? Is it his or her voice? Is it his or her mannerisms? Is it his or her stern look or domineering attitude?" Once you have answered these questions, you can ask yourself: "Of whom does this person remind me? Is it my father or mother? Is it my uncle or aunt? Is it my older or younger brother or sister? Is it a teacher or a priest? Is it a friend?" As soon as you have identified the person from whom you are "transferring" the attributes you find distasteful, you can ask a further question: "What are the differences between this acquaintance who is getting on my nerves and the person in my past life?" If you do this each time the acquaintance annoys you, you may well begin to feel less uncomfortable in his or her presence. In this way, you also get to know more about the history of your emotion of annoyance.

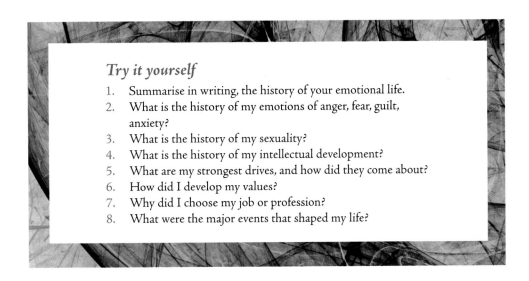

Try it yourself

1. Summarise in writing, the history of your emotional life.
2. What is the history of my emotions of anger, fear, guilt, anxiety?
3. What is the history of my sexuality?
4. What is the history of my intellectual development?
5. What are my strongest drives, and how did they come about?
6. How did I develop my values?
7. Why did I choose my job or profession?
8. What were the major events that shaped my life?

Dreams: getting to know our personal shadow – all that we have repressed

Some people are very sceptical about dream work; they don't believe it will help them in any way to discover the truth about themselves. I would have thought the same about fifty years ago; I would have laughed at a person who wanted to help me find a relevant, personal meaning in a dream. As I studied Sigmund Freud, Carl Jung, Fritz Perls, Calvin S. Hall, Ann Faraday and many other authors who have written about dream work, I began to write down my own dreams and look at them. I got more and more interested in dream work. Since then I have worked on hundreds of my own dreams and found them extremely useful for obtaining insights into myself; I have helped hundreds of others to find profound meaning in their dreams.

So I would like to introduce you to some of the techniques and therapeutic reasoning involved in this work, and I would ask you, if you are sceptical, to try to explore your dreams in the ways suggested; it is a path to healing almost as old as recorded human history.

The old Israel, the Mesopotamians, and the Egyptians used dream work to find out what they should do in given situations. In the Old Testament there are many passages about dreams, and there were several famous dream interpreters like Joseph and Daniel. Several dreams are mentioned in the New Testament, particularly in the nativity stories. Even early Christianity used dream work to find out God's will for them. Then dream work virtually disappeared for many centuries. Freud and Jung started a revival. Nowadays, dream work is very much part of the therapeutic approach to finding out more about our unconscious.

Many discoveries have been made due to dreams. They are creative agents. Albert Einstein developed his theory of relativity due to a dream he had as an adolescent. In this dream he was riding on a sledge. The sledge accelerated, going faster and faster until it approached the speed of light. The stars began to distort into amazing patterns and colours, dazzling him with the beauty and power of their transformation. He said that in many ways, his entire scientific career could have been seen as an extended meditation on that dream.

Fredrick Kekule discovered the molecular structure of benzene that he had been trying to define for years, in a dream as he slept in a chair one afternoon. In this dream he saw a snake with its tail in its mouth. From this he realised that benzene was a closed ring of carbon molecules. He was so taken by the nature of his discovery that at the research conference he urged his colleagues, "Gentlemen, learn to dream."

Some people say that they never dream. They may not remember their dreams. Most of us dream five times a night. Why do we not remember these dreams? There are many reasons for this. Part of the reason is that we do not consider them important. We may even regard them as nonsense. They are not: dreams and nightmares bring up feelings which we find difficult to cope with. This may be another reason why we do not remember them. We try to repress painful things and keep them out of awareness. However, they still disturb us in many ways.

What are some of the ways we can help ourselves to remember our dreams? We need to be motivated to remember them. We will be motivated if we consider them as useful tools for our personal growth. Say to yourself before you fall asleep, "Tonight I will remember my dreams"; "I will wake up after I have had a dream and record it." Put an exercise book next to the bed, to record the dream. You can also visualise yourself waking up and recording the dream. Do not dismiss any fragment of a dream as being unimportant. The biggest incentive for remembering dreams is to share them with somebody who is interested in dream work.

Dream work is the door to the unconscious. With their assistance we can find out what our unconscious contains. A dream is like a letter: we receive it, open and read it, and then respond to it. Once we have received a dream in our sleep, we need to open it to find the meaning of the dream, and then to respond to it. This is dream work.

The first step in dream work is to write down the dream in detail, without censoring it. We need to write down all the characters, animals, things, colours, feelings, thoughts, values, actions that appear in the dream. They can all be highly meaningful. This written report is the first technique for revealing meaning in the dream.

The dreamer can then use further techniques to discover the meaning of a dream. These techniques focus on re-experiencing the feelings and images of the dream. In this way, by working with the feelings, meaning will spontaneously arise. The dreamer will recognise connections. Often dreams refer to areas of growth such as becoming more patient, less anxious, more assertive, more understanding, more compassionate.

Try it yourself

Part 1

When doing dream work ask the following questions: "What title would suit the dream?"; "What themes appear in it?"; "What actions are there?"; "What feelings are revealed?"; "What central questions does the dream appear to be asking itself within its scenario?" Then, a little more objectively, ask yourself:

♦ What important questions with regard to the dream do I perceive?

♦ What is the meaning of the dream?

♦ What does the dream want to teach me?

♦ What can I learn from the dream?

♦ What are its main messages for my life, work and future?

Part 2

Dreams are full of symbols: locations, animals, objects like windows, seas, rivers, doors, waves, sky, meadow, trees. You can have a dialogue with any of these dream symbols as if you were conversing with a person. It is best to "converse" with what appears to be the most significant symbol in the dream: "why are you in my dream?"; "What do you represent from my life?" Ask the symbol questions, but allow the answers to come up from deep within yourself.

Part 3

After writing down your dream and doing the basic dream work, re-read the dream. Try to notice the various actions and attitudes taken by the dream ego, that is, by you and other figures in the dream. Ask yourself the questions: "What am I doing in my dream?"; "What are my attitudes?"; "What alternatives are there for the way it develops?"

Now take three pieces of paper and write on each of them a single question:

1. *What am I doing?* Under this heading, write down in sequence the things that are done by all the figures in the dream. Assume that the figures are all aspects of yourself. What did anyone say, do or choose?

2. *What are my attitudes?* Write down the attitudes and feelings of every character in the dream.

3. *Alternatives.* On this page write your reflections on the actions and attitudes. You can ask yourself the following questions: "Are the behaviour patterns and attitudes in the dream similar to those of my waking state?"; "Am I satisfied with the way I act or react in the dream, or would I like to change my behaviour and my reactions?" If there is something you would like to change, make a note next to the action or attitude. Generate as many possible alternatives as you can. Then reflect on these contrasts, and ask yourself what you have learnt.

Lucid dreams

"Lucid dreams" is a term that refers to that sudden state of awareness we sometimes experience in a dream, when we know that we are dreaming. Ask yourself what the sudden awareness implies. Lucid dreams as a resource can help actively with children. They should make friends with the monsters in the dream, or, on waking, they can be invited to imagine that one of their parents is with them in the dream. For children, there is less distinction between dreaming and waking, so they can easily carry over such suggestions into their dreams and be less frightened when they have a nightmare.

"Dream incubation" means that we prepare ourselves to have a certain kind of dream before we go to sleep. The ancient Greeks used this kind of technique. They visited the temple in Epidaurus for healing dreams. Their preparation consisted in fasting and certain rituals. This technique is also used by Native Americans to get "big" dreams. How can we use it? We can write about a problem we would like help with. We do this just before going to bed. We look at all the issues relevant to the problem: How long have I had it? What have I tried to do about it? What do I hope to gain by solving it? Now ask for a dream that will give you a representation of the problem. Do not ask for a solution. We must not use this method for trivial things as we need to be patient in waiting for answers.

How can we apply all these techniques to a particular dream?

Here are three actual dreams recounted by a therapist; we shall call them "The dreams of a group counsellor":

Dream report 1

"Several of us are in the kitchen washing up. There are many dishes to be washed up. I am doing the washing up. Others are there watching me. I can't get on with the job. I don't know where to put the dishes. I have been washing up for a long time. There is still a lot to be done. It seems I am not making much progress. The people round me don't seem to be helping."

What title does the dream want to give itself?	There is too much work.
Themes	Washing up; no help; not much progress; where to put the dishes.
Emotions	Overwhelmed; anxious; discouraged.
Questions	Dream, what do you want to tell or teach me?
Answers	Your therapeutic work is infinite. Don't worry even if you do not see the progress. There are many small steps in all this. Some people simply can't help you. Don't get discouraged.

Dream report 2

"I am going into a meeting room. There are only three members of the group there. I am disappointed and disheartened. I tell the three to go and get the others, because I am about to give a talk, and they may miss something that is important to them."

What title does the dream want to give to itself?	Empty lecture room.
Themes	Empty room, few members.
Emotions	Disappointed, disheartened.
Questions	Dream, what do you want to tell me? Dream, what is your message for me? Dream, what do I need to learn from you?
Answers	There is a lot of undermining going on in your counselling group. You need to counter that. Remind them of the ground rules established when the group first started.

Dream report 3

"I dreamt, almost abstractly, that the Greeks believed that those who trust themselves can achieve what they want to achieve. I had formerly seen this proverb in a book, and it came to me again while I was asleep."

What title does the dream want to give to itself?	Trust in yourself.
Themes	Greek philosophers, belief, trust, achievement.
Emotions	Happy, excited.
Questions	Dream, what do you want to tell me?
Answer	You can achieve, whatever you trust yourself to achieve.

If we take the three dreams in order, we can see a progression. The first one shows the counsellor's feeling of being overwhelmed with the amount of work to be done in the group. The second dream points to some of the members spoiling the atmosphere. The third dream encourages the counsellor to carry on although the work is hard. You can see the sequence of the three dreams. Only the dreamer can ultimately find the meaning of his or her dreams.

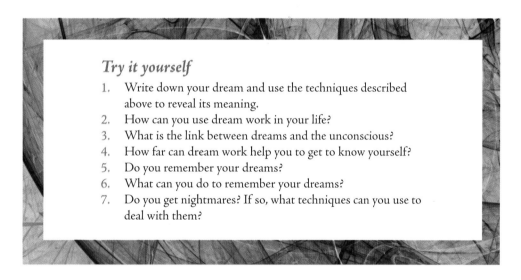

Try it yourself

1. Write down your dream and use the techniques described above to reveal its meaning.
2. How can you use dream work in your life?
3. What is the link between dreams and the unconscious?
4. How far can dream work help you to get to know yourself?
5. Do you remember your dreams?
6. What can you do to remember your dreams?
7. Do you get nightmares? If so, what techniques can you use to deal with them?

Finally, be patient with your dreams. Do not try to interpret them until meanings become apparent.

Learning to forgive ourselves for all the mistakes we have made

One of the most difficult things to do is to forgive ourselves for the mistakes we have made. Many people carry guilt-feelings for years and years. The biggest mistake we make is not to forgive ourselves. Everybody makes mistakes; we can learn from them and then forgive ourselves and move on. Not forgiving ourselves is a form of anger towards ourselves. It is a punishment. It is self-hatred. This is an unnecessarily heavy burden for us to carry.

Learning to forgive ourselves is important for our mental health. Many things can help us to forgive ourselves. We ask our Lord in the Our Father to forgive us and we know that he forgives us when we repent for our sins and shortcomings. We can learn to imitate our Lord in this process of forgiveness. When we forgive others we do not cling on to hurts inflicted on us and we may learn to forgive ourselves. If we grow in forgiving others, we may find it easier to forgive ourselves. As we learn to forgive ourselves, we grow in love for ourselves. This is part of the great commandment: "Love your neighbour as yourself."

It is good for children to learn, as part of family life, to forgive themselves when they make mistakes. Parents, teachers and priests can help them to achieve this. Not forgiving ourselves wastes a lot of energy. The mass media could be a powerful force to get across the message that people need to learn to forgive themselves.

An unforgiving religion or society is a big burden for everybody to carry and it is totally unnecessary and highly destructive. It blocks the flow of energy in people. What is important is that we learn from our mistakes. Once we learn from mistakes, the mistake can turn into a blessing, because it has enriched us and others.

Think of St Peter who denied Jesus. Jesus forgave him, because Peter had grown in love for Jesus. Jesus chose him and named him as the rock on which he would build his Church. Human society may not forgive you the mistakes you have made. However, God will forgive you and you can become great in God's eyes, as Peter did. Saul persecuted the Christians. When Jesus appeared to him and challenged him, he repented for having persecuted Christians and became the greatest missionary of all times. Jesus forgave Mary Magdalene all her sins because she showed great love for him.

Humility, as spiritual writers tell us, is one of the central virtues for us human beings on our spiritual journey; pride is the great obstacle to spiritual growth. It is difficult for us to acquire virtues. Often we learn them the hard way, by making mistakes.

When children make a mistake, we, as parents and teachers, point it out to them, but we must not withdraw our love for them. In fact, we need to go out of our way to show our love for them, because the child will feel bad after having made a mistake. When parents and teachers are no longer stuck in the mistake the child has made, the child will follow suit and gradually learn to forgive him- or herself and then move on.

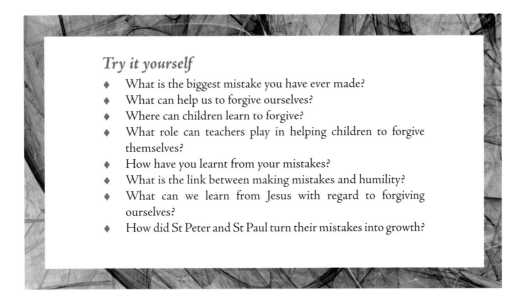

Try it yourself

♦ What is the biggest mistake you have ever made?

♦ What can help us to forgive ourselves?

♦ Where can children learn to forgive?

♦ What role can teachers play in helping children to forgive themselves?

♦ How have you learnt from your mistakes?

♦ What is the link between making mistakes and humility?

♦ What can we learn from Jesus with regard to forgiving ourselves?

♦ How did St Peter and St Paul turn their mistakes into growth?

Learning to forgive others who have hurt us

It is important for human beings to learn to forgive each other. People will hurt each other without intending it when they live together. They may say or do something which hurts the other person. Therefore, we need to learn to forgive each other. Otherwise human relationships become an unbearable burden. Each act of forgiveness is an act of love. Each time we forgive, we grow in love. Each time we forgive, it becomes easier to forgive.

Why should we forgive? Forgiveness means letting go and moving towards the person who hurt us. A person who forgives must release the resentment, bitterness, hatred, the desire to seek revenge.

Some people would say: "Don't forgive!" They may give their reasons: "Forgiveness obstructs justice"; forgiveness makes no difference to the legal crime. "If you forgive, you are being cowardly"; on the contrary, it is harder to forgive than to hate. It takes much courage to forgive.

Through his own life Jesus taught us the lesson of forgiveness. He came into the world to bring us back to his Father and reconcile us with him. God forgave us. He taught us to forgive and to forgive again and again. Jesus instructed the disciples to pray: "Forgive us our debts as we also have forgiven our debtors." This is so important for healthy human relationships. Without forgiving one another, life is unbearable. The lack of forgiveness is a very heavy burden to carry. People are healthier and happier if they forgive. When we forgive, we feel free and we can move on with life. Bitterness poisons our whole organism.

If we think that we, too, have hurt other people, it may help us to forgive others. How glad we are when others whom we have hurt forgive us. Can we not give this gift of forgiveness to others who hurt us?

What happens in a family where the members do not forgive each other the hurts they have inflicted? They avoid each other. They do not look at each other. They do not talk to each other. There is an atmosphere of cold war. The family members feel lonely, isolated, hurt and withdrawn. Their relationships suffer or break down altogether.

We can distinguish between making a decision to forgive and forgiving emotionally. A friend might say: "I forgot your birthday. Can you forgive me?" Without hesitation the other person replies: "Of course, I forgive you." This is an act of the will. Emotional forgiveness is part of a process that takes much longer. When we get hurt, we experience the feelings of fear and anger. Both block the relationship with the offending person. We may be afraid that we will be hurt again, so we cling on to the hurt and avoid the person. Emotional forgiveness changes the heart. In emotional forgiveness we replace the hot emotions of anger and fear with empathy, love and compassion.

How can we achieve emotional forgiveness? Our hurtful memories are not wiped out. We remember them differently after we forgive. Hate, bitterness and resentment are replaced with positive thoughts and feelings. The memory of hurt remains, but it is associated with different emotions. When we achieve complete forgiveness, friendship is substituted for hostility. When we forgive, we replace the emotional attachment to the transgression: we reduce the negative emotions and increase the positive emotions.

Try it yourself

Healing forgiveness will not occur until your emotions change. For this to happen, try to recall the hurt and pray for healing. Be sensitive to the leading of the Holy Spirit. Watch that you do not slip into rage, fear or depression and get stuck in them. However, you do need to feel your anger and fear and whatever emotion is linked with it. This is a first recall of the event of hurt. Then you can recall it again. This time try to replace the negative emotions with more positive emotions. Try this time to be more objective. You must not be afraid to express some negative emotions, but try to keep them under control. Try to remember what you felt about what was happening, and use precise "feeling" words like "angry", "afraid", "anxious", "furious", "deeply hurt". You may struggle to get the precise words that best describe your feelings. You will probably find that thinking of such words will take some of the hurtful edge off the memory.

As you recall the hurt, take deep, slow breaths to keep yourself calm. Be sure to exhale fully. If you empty your lungs, inhaling will take care of itself. Calming breaths help you to remember objectively. Now try to understand why the perpetrator did what he or she did. If you can light that spark of positive feeling – empathy, compassion, love – it can blaze into forgiveness.

Some people ruminate over a hurt and become unforgiving. The anger and fear become less, however other emotions become stronger: resentment, bitterness, hatred, hostility. How can a person reach emotional forgiveness? The person needs to work through these emotions and try to understand the person who has given them pain and replace these emotions with understanding and love. Jesus taught us to love our enemies and to do good to those who hate us. When we don't behave in this way, a cycle of revenge sets in and becomes terribly destructive. We see this most clearly when nations declare war against each other. Yes, it is difficult to forgive our enemies. But if we do not forgive them, we destroy ourselves by fostering hatred, revenge and resentment. We ruin our own health.

Learning from past experiences

We can all learn from past experiences. This is the normal human experience, beginning with the toddler learning to walk and talk, who experiences many failures before success is reached. With the support of others the child learns many skills by practising them. It is much the same with adolescents and adults.

Some of us, however, seem not to learn much from past experiences. It may be that we learnt the opposite behaviour that is deeply ingrained in us and can only be changed when we have become aware of it and have the support of others to change it. We commit the same mistake again and again. Counsellors and friends can help us in this process of learning from past experiences.

So it is normal to make mistakes; it is part of our human condition. However we can learn from all past mistakes. We may have failed in an examination, because we did not prepare ourselves for it. Now as we reflect on this past experience, we decide to prepare ourselves better in the future. A relationship may have failed because we always insisted on our own opinion. As we reflect on this failure, we decide to learn to listen to the other person in the future and become a more integrated person.

- A student realises that she cannot study in the evening, because she feels too tired. So she decides to study in the morning.
- A teacher feels depressed and miserable when it rains. Then he realises that he does not get enough physical exercise, because he is always in the classroom or marking. He decides to go for a walk after school, even when it is raining.
- A very nervous person finds out that when she meditates, she feels calm. She decides to meditate every day.
- A mother, whose ten-year-old son is in hospital with a serious illness, decides to pray in desperation. She experiences deep peace and decides to resume her prayer life.
- A father is told by his wife that he does not love his children. First he feels a lot of anger because he does indeed love them. He feels hurt that his wife would say that to him. As he keeps on reflecting, he realises that perhaps he is not good at expressing his love for his children. He decides to remedy that in different ways. He spends more time with them. He takes them for a walk, and listens to their stories. Now he is much happier, because the children respond to him, and his wife notices how the situation has improved.

Try it yourself

Write short answers to these questions without referring to a previous section:

♦ Why should I forgive those who have hurt me?
♦ What does Jesus teach us with regard to forgiving?
♦ What happens in families where members do not forgive each other?
♦ What happens in communities where people do not forgive each other?
♦ What is the difference between decisional and emotional forgiveness?
♦ What happens when we ruminate over hurts inflicted on us?
♦ What can help me to understand the person who has made me suffer?
♦ How does it affect my health, when I do not forgive?

The following things can help you to empathise with a speaker:

♦ Underneath any attack is often a sense of fear, stress, worry and hurt. When a person attacks you, picture the person as needy, weak and afraid.
♦ When you understand that people react strongly to certain situations, it can help you to understand them and forgive them.

- Very often people don't think things through when they are hurt. They just want to lash out.
- People who hurt us often do so because they have been conditioned by past experiences in childhood.
- Prayer will help us to understand the person who hurt us and motivate us to forgive. Writing down the story of the event of hurt from the viewpoint of the perpetrator may help us to understand that person.
- Set up two chairs in a private place. Pretend that one chair is occupied by the person who hurt you. Sit in the other chair. By switching chairs and talking for each person, you might become more understanding, empathic and loving towards the perpetrator.

Make notes on these questions:
- What do we need to do when we make mistakes?
- Give illustrations of how you have learnt from your mistakes.
- Who can help you to learn from past experiences?
- Are there still areas in your life where you need to learn from past experiences? How will you go about this?
- Write a few paragraphs describing a toddler learning to walk and talk.

Conclusions

As we get to know ourselves better, we have more choice in what we say and do. We no longer do so many things we later regret. As we learn to forgive ourselves and others, we will experience more peace in ourselves and bring that peace to our family, to our community, our work place and church, and to our society as a whole. We shall discover a positive energy in all these places. As we learn from the past, we will be able to avoid mistakes and failures, and to experience more freedom in our lives.

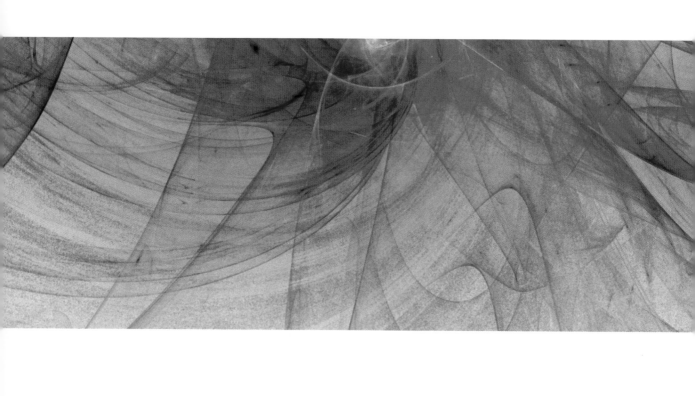

Chapter five

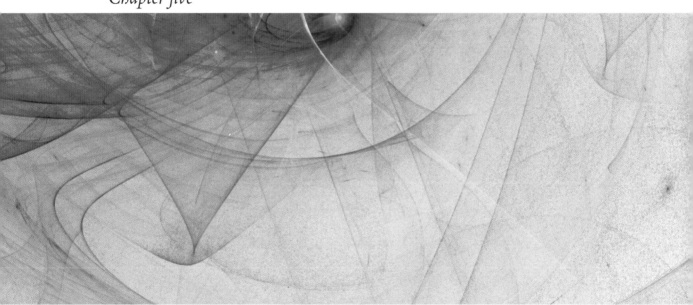

Learning to live a healthy life

Developing self-esteem

Without self-esteem it is hard even to understand why it is good to be healthy. As we have previously described, self-esteem can only develop if we turn our inner voice into a loving, nurturing parent, and do away with generalisations like, "I am no good"; "I am stupid"; "I never do anything right"; "I always fail in relationships." We can become more specific about ourselves, and let all the good points about ourselves come into our awareness and hold on to them. We can find out from whom we learnt to feel bad about ourselves, and who our negative role models were. We can try to let go of negative self-criticism.

Try it yourself

Part 1

1. Imagine your internal destructive critic is in front of you. You are the adult confronting this destructive critic. State the truth about yourself. Let your emotions come into this. Tell the critic that you do not need his or her approval, because you approve of yourself. Try to stop identifying with each of your negative role models, while keeping the positive identifications.

2. Start nurturing your inner child as a good parent would do. A good parent would show love, compassion, acceptance, respect, support and encouragement. Learn what feels nurturing for you. Take time and ask yourself, "Being nurtured: what is that like for me?" Afterwards, describe on paper as accurately as possible those things that contributed to you feeling nurtured. When you next have some spare time, read the list over again, slowly and carefully. Your inner child is expressing its needs. Listen. Little by little, you will learn to communicate empathically with your inner child.

Part 2

Answer these general questions, if possible in conjunction with a friend or colleague who also agrees to answer them:

- How can we develop self-esteem?
- How and why did we develop self-criticism?
- What is the role of patience in the process of developing our self-esteem?

Taking enough physical exercise

Many people who would like to live a healthy life do not know how to go about it. They live according to the unhealthy ways they learnt while they were growing up. Some spend most of their free time watching programmes on TV. Others spend long hours playing computer games. Their sitting room has become a storeroom, their bedroom a television room. Their garden is a wilderness. They eat food that takes as little time as possible to prepare. They like to drink a can or two of beer every night and they enjoy parties, but they hardly ever go for a walk; they are not used to it. They often complain that they are not feeling well. The doctor tells them that there is nothing physically wrong with them. Nevertheless, there is something wrong.

We all need physical exercise. Our muscles must be exercised and physical exercise helps our digestive system. Some people go regularly for a swim which keeps them fit, others play football. Some work out in the gym, others go for walks. Some people run a few miles a day. Jogging has become a sport for many. Fishing is one of the main types of sport in the country. Many people enjoy working in the garden. However, there are just as many others who do not really accept that they need physical exercise, even though they do not feel well. They are so used to not feeling well, that the feeling has become habitual. Their doctors may or may not prescribe medication, but their basic problem has not been looked at.

Particularly for people with fairly sedentary lives or occupations, it is necessary for their health that they take time for physical exercise in whatever form is best for them. Without that, they will soon feel that they are not well. It is basically a lack of movement. Our bodies need physical exercise. Because we do not use many of our muscles to their full capacity, we slowly lose much of our flexibility and end up in old age scarcely able to move.

Have you ever thought about the way you move about? We learnt early on that without effort we won't get anywhere in life. We were probably told this endlessly. Now we need to let ourselves discard unnecessary effort and discover how easy and gentle things can be. Once this attitude permeates our unconscious mind, we will be more relaxed in what we do.

You can ask yourself the following questions: "Am I standing up straight?"; "Am I leaning forward?"; "Am I leaning backward?" If we are leaning forward or backward, where does the lean start from? Does it start from the ankles? Does it start from the hips? Does it start from the upper back or shoulders? Unbalanced posture can put a strain on the skeletal system and the internal organs. You may have heard about the Alexander Technique. Many ideas concerning posture come from Frederick Alexander who experimented with his posture in front of mirrors to discover how he held his body. He noticed that he had acquired bad habits that interfered with his performance of reciting Shakespeare's great speeches. He learnt some fascinating lessons.

Alexander talked about inhibition – that is, stopping for one moment before we do anything. This gives us time to use our reasoning power. It enables us to decide upon the most efficient way of performing an action. This applies to any movement we make. For example, we can choose the best way of bending down to pick up something, and so avoid back pain. Inhibition is the practice of pausing before an action. In this way we stop our habitual reactions, we break our bad habits.

The next step is to give ourselves conscious directions. Alexander formulated the directions: "Let the neck be free so that the head can go forward and up, so that the back can lengthen and widen." These conscious instructions enable the body to release, lengthen and widen.

Improving our ordinary posture

Good posture is not easily found. The way we hold our body is the result of many past experiences; we become enslaved to certain postures and we do not realise that the rigid shape we have acquired is unnatural. A depressed person's physique tends to collapse, and he or she might suffer less if the body were held in a more upright manner while walking, sitting or standing up.

A child moves freely and naturally in the early years. The four-year-old is upright in a natural and effortless way; the teenager is much more slumped. For a start, holding the body still at a desk for long periods of time causes the tiring and tensing of many muscles.

We can improve our standing position. How can we do that? The feet can be at 45-degree angle with about nine inches between them. This provides us with a solid base for the rest of the body. One foot can be placed slightly behind the other. The weight of the body can rest mainly on the rear foot. This prevents us from slipping down onto one hip. Sinking down onto one hip affects the balance of the whole structure. We must allow the hips to go back without altering the balance and without throwing the body forward. This prevents us from pushing the pelvis forward.

Developing a nicely poised sitting position means that we neither slump nor sit up rigidly. When we stand up, we should not thrust our bodies forward, ejecting them with the use of the arms of the chair; rather, we lean forward from the hips, and gently rise. When we sit, we should maintain a reasonably upright posture, and not slump down like a sack of potatoes.

It is important to keep these instructions of Alexander in mind when we take physical exercise. Exercise can improve overall physical health and can also improve our mental health. It is very important for older people. Walking can improve abilities such as learning, abstract reasoning and concentration. It is the best antidepressant. Start off with moderate exercise, and gradually increase it. Walk your way to health. Do the exercise you most enjoy. You can even enjoy housework as a form of exercise! Do not overdo anything. Addiction to exercise can cause injury.

Breathing properly

Some of us have acquired a habit of breathing in a shallow way. When we sit for a long time, we are inclined to breathe in a sluggish way. We do not exhale properly. This affects our whole system negatively. Poor breathing can bring on aches and pains, and bad headaches.

If you ask someone to breathe deeply they will most likely raise their shoulders up and arch their back. This breathing may feel deep, but it is not. Correct breathing is essential to health. The body needs to receive enough oxygen so we need to breathe efficiently and deeply. Our lungs are situated in the ribcage. By expanding the ribcage, the volume of the cavity is increased and so the cavity for oxygen intake is increased. This type of breathing exercises the muscles between the ribs. It expands the ribs. It makes the upper body more mobile. The lungs become like bellows. The lower ribcage expands as you breathe in; it closes down as you breathe out.

Shallow breathing will affect the whole system as oxygen is needed by every organ in the body. To function well, we need energy. The chemical reaction that turns the food we eat into energy requires oxygen. Oxygen is received from the air by means of the lungs. The lungs expand and draw in air through the nose. Alexander became known as the "breathing man." He acquired an ability to breathe effortlessly and noiselessly when he acted or recited.

Through the practice of the Alexander Technique a greater quantity of air is inspired into and expelled from the lungs. The oxygenation of the blood is more adequate and the digestive system more stimulated. The action of the heart improves, and this all leads to better health.

Try it yourself

- ♦ What forms of physical exercise do I enjoy?
- ♦ How does the lack of physical exercise affect me?
- ♦ What happens when I do not use some of my muscles?
- ♦ How do I ordinarily move about, sit and stand?
- ♦ What kind of questions will help me to check on my posture?
- ♦ What have I learnt about the Alexander Technique?
- ♦ What is inhibition according to the Alexander Technique?
- ♦ What can I do to improve my breathing?

Go for a long walk, and then write about the physical experience.

Eating enough healthy food

I always say that we must have enough food: healthy food and well-cooked food. Some people do not eat enough. I expect my own experience is very common. For years I listened to people advising me about what I should eat, because I always felt weak and tired. Some would say that when I felt tired, I should take sugar. Yes, it may help my immediate tiredness, but it will produce long-term misery! Another piece of advice was not to eat any meat. I tried it out for six months and felt I was getting worse. Not all of us can be vegetarians, even though we might wish to be.

When I came to England, I worked with someone who really knew about diet. She told me to eat everything, including at least a little of the food I did not particularly like. She encouraged me to eat more fresh vegetables. The larger the variety the more likely we are to have all the minerals and nutrients we need. My health improved enormously as a result of this instruction.

Diet has a major effect on our health, and lots of fruit and vegetables can improve it. When we eat, our blood sugar level goes up. When we use energy, our blood sugar level goes down. When our blood sugar is too low, we feel tired or irritable, because the cells do not get what they need. When the blood pressure is too high, it also has a negative impact on our health. Fats are important for the proper functioning and structure of the brain. Therefore, not all fat is to be avoided. Some fats are even to be encouraged. Fish, we are told, is the best brain food. Herbs have been used for medicinal purposes for centuries. It is healthy to keep to regular meal times.

Once, a religious sister, who had lots of allergies and could hardly eat anything which was provided for her meals, came to see me. The manager of the kitchen wanted to send her away. She complained that she had to buy her own food and cook it. She kept on talking about how her sisters in her community told her that there was nothing wrong with her. Even the doctor told her that it was all in her mind. As she told me all this, I realised that the food had become a means of getting attention. I challenged her, saying, "I think you are playing a dangerous game. My suspicion is that you have cornered yourself into getting attention by convincing yourself that you have all these allergies." I said to her: "Tonight, try to eat whatever is placed on the table.

However, chew it properly and eat just a little bit." Next day she told me that she no longer had a problem! I said, "You are quite capable of getting the attention you need in more constructive ways."

On the other hand, there are people who do have serious allergies; we can develop them at any point in our lives. If we are not sure, we should see a doctor. There is a multitude of men and women who over-eat in compensation for psychological needs. They may feel a lack of love, security and appreciation and try to compensate by eating. Counselling can help people learn the psychological skills needed to make sure their basic needs are satisfied so that they do not need to compensate by overeating.

Drink enough, but not excessively

Some people do not drink enough liquid. Others drink too much alcohol, or other drinks that may be high in caffeine or sugar. We become unhealthy when we take too much. While it is important to be hospitable, we should be wary of pressurising people to drink more than they may wish.

In certain situations, as when there is inflammation, we should drink a lot of liquid to wash the toxins out of the system, so that they do not spread from one place in the body to another. Many people do not drink enough water, which is essential for healthy living.

If somebody has a problem with sweet drinks or alcohol, it is good for that person to ask him- or herself, "What is the underlying need I try to compensate for?"; "Do I look for love, for security, for appreciation?"; "How can I get these needs met in a more constructive way?" If I am addicted to alcohol, I probably need professional help; but I can start by detaching myself, by telling myself, "I am more than just an alcoholic". I can start to regain my power, so that I can gain control over my drinking habits. Any addiction ruins our life and does not lead to happiness and a better future. If we want to move forward into a better future, we can help by addressing our addiction problems.

Try it yourself

♦ Should you encourage people to drink alcohol?
♦ What are some of the mistakes we make with regard to drinking?
♦ What do you need to do when you have an inflammation?
♦ What would you say to a person who has a drinking problem?
♦ What do we need to do with addiction problems?
♦ What is the relationship between addiction and need fulfilment?
♦ How much liquid do you believe you need to drink every day?
♦ How can a person with a drinking problem start to help him- or herself?

Draw up a list of your eating and drinking habits. Do you wish to change anything?

Spending time every day in silence, prayer, meditation and reflection

Our relationship with God is the most fundamental relationship, because he created us. Nothing does more damage to society and each individual than the denial of this most basic relationship – the basis of our existence. Once we accept that God exists, it has many fundamental consequences for our way of living, values and the nature of true happiness. Therefore we have to nourish the relationship constantly and lay solid foundations for our whole life and well-being. How can we learn to be still, to keep silence, to pray and meditate? Our desire is to become like God, who is love. We aim every day to become Christ-like by growing in love. We do not always succeed in growing in love, but we continue our efforts daily. Stillness, silence, prayer and meditation assist us in this spiritual journey towards union with God. They calm the whole system down. Particularly in this age of stress in which we live, we need to calm down from time to time to give our organism a chance to recover.

Prayer raises our mind, heart and will to God, and it connects us with God. Jesus himself spent nights in prayer to keep connected with his Father in heaven. What food is for the body prayer is for the soul.

Mass is at the centre of our Catholic life: it unites us with Christ. It encourages us to live as he did. It constantly nourishes us in the meal and the word of God. This strength which we receive in the Eucharist helps us to carry on our work, however difficult it may prove, and however old we may be.

Try it yourself

Pointers for a meditation

1. How do I foster my relationship with God?
2. What does my relationship with God do to my daily life?
3. What parts do stillness, silence, prayer and meditation play in my life?
4. What part does prayer play in my life? What can prayer do?
5. What is the role of the Eucharist in my life?

Stimulating one's intellect through reading and studying

It is important that we keep on reading to keep updated, and to exercise our intellect and memory. Reading keeps us informed of what is going on in society and in the world. It creates an interest that is energising. Obviously different people will read different books. It depends on their area of interest.

Studying is an activity that can bring us much joy. We can use a variety of different methods. For example one may simply read and re-read a textbook, or one can underline the main points and important details in the text. Somebody else may read a page or two, and then make brief outline notes.

A common difficulty with study is having no clear plan and timetable. Many students just muddle along. They do a bit of this subject or that, leaving it to their mood. Some let the books pile up. Try to develop a plan and timetable for studying. We can study better at some times than at others. Some study more fruitfully in the morning, others find it more useful to study in the late evening, after something to eat.

Try it yourself
- What methods do you use for studying a textbook?
- What might a clearer plan and timetable do for your reading or studies?

Getting enough sleep

We spend a third of our time sleeping. What does sleep do for us? It offers us refuge from unpleasant events. We spend two hours a night dreaming. During this time our brain processes old memories. Our brain and body need deep sleep to recover from the day. We are much more alert when we have had enough sleep.

When we sleep, we let go of the tension of the day. Sleep is a temporary ceasefire from arguments. Sleep is essential for health so it's important to make sure we get sufficient. Tired people are vulnerable and less emotionally resilient. They often feel out of touch with what happens around them. Sleep deprivation can lead to feelings of depression. It impairs performance and damages social relationships.

Some people find it very difficult to go to bed and therefore delay it till the early hours in the morning. They may have a drink and watch TV. They may have become prisoners of the computer and computer games or slaves of pornography. We all need to learn a certain discipline. We are not meant to work at night and sleep by day. Many people have to do so, and need to find their own way of turning the normal sleep pattern on its head without becoming disorientated.

Sleepiness can cause accidents and injuries. If our sleep is poor for a long period of time, it may even damage the immune system, so that we become more susceptible to infection. People who habitually go to bed earlier tend to live longer.

Looking after one's body

Our bodies are a great gift, to be looked after and cared for. St Francis apologised to his body for the way he had treated it. The Blessed Trinity dwells in us, and so our bodies are to be treasured. The Latin proverb *Mens sana in corpore sano* means "a healthy mind in a healthy body". Regular visits to the doctor and dentist help us keep our bodies healthy, and keeping them clean by washing daily, having a bath or a shower, is important.

When I dress properly, I show respect for my body. Some people take great care to dress nicely while others do not bother much. How we dress affects our self-esteem. It is another way of showing love for ourselves, which is part of the great commandment. In German there is a proverb which states, *Kleider machen Menschen* which means, "clothes make people."

Whatever happens to us, it will have its effect on our bodies. All of us have had experiences that make us withdraw. These experiences include being reprimanded by teachers, parents, employers and others. They also include being ridiculed by friends and members of our peer group, or rejection by loved ones. If these experiences happen frequently, we will eventually become strongly introverted, and we may develop a posture that shows a defensive attitude. This posture remains long after the experiences of rejection, ridicule and reprimand. A defensive posture is easy to identify in hunched or rounded shoulders, a collapsed torso and much tension in the neck muscles.

Learning to undo the damage done to our bodies by working through all the upsetting emotions that still linger in them from the past can help us. It means going back to the various events and going back into the emotions that accompanied them, allowing these toxic emotions to be removed from our system. In this process our muscles may become loosened, our bodies more flexible.

Try it yourself

- ♦ What is my responsibility regarding my body?
- ♦ How do I look after my body?
- ♦ What happens to my body when I withdraw?
- ♦ How can I show respect for my body?
- ♦ How are past events registered in my body?
- ♦ Do I need to change some of my physical habits?
- ♦ What does working through my emotions do to my body?

Socialising

We are social beings and therefore mixing with people is important. By being with people we may receive energy and we can learn much from each other. Family, friends, colleagues and people in general make life rich. We may need to cultivate relationships and spend less time in our offices. We talk a lot about our priorities. Sometimes we neglect the people we are closest to until a crisis arises. We must not wait for a disaster to happen before we open our hearts to those who are closest to us. We can start today. For many of us, there is also the need to withdraw from company. This can provide another kind of energy.

Make a list of the people you are close to: family, friends, colleagues, neighbours. Who are the people who make your life what it is? Doctors, dentists, priests, plumbers, journalists? Ask yourself: "What do I need to change to find more time for others?" People find many excuses not to change. "I may lose my job, if I spend more time with my family. If I lose my job, my family will suffer." Losing a job is a common fear in a time of unemployment, but the fear is not always the reality.

How can I make myself more available, without becoming a doormat? This is the tension in all relationships. To come close to others we have to loosen our boundaries, but if we dissolve them completely we may fall into codependency. Spending more time with others helps us to deepen emotional bonds and to maintain healthy boundaries. We create boundaries by saying "no" without feeling guilt or the fear of rejection. If we have neglected a relationship, we may compensate by becoming too self-sacrificing. Then we can become resentful. It is difficult to undo an exploitive relationship. Therefore, watch that your relationship does not become exploitive. Maintaining healthy boundaries is essential for building loving

relationships. Children need boundaries. Many people do not learn boundaries in their families and get into trouble later in life. In counselling, one of the most important aspects is to help clients to develop healthy boundaries.

We are interconnected with all human beings. We can reach out to everybody: friend and stranger. We can delight in our differences and at the same time feel closer to those who are our relatives and friends. We can hold our own opinion, without belittling others.

Shy people may find it very difficult to socialise with other people; others find it difficult to be alone, only feeling at ease when they are with people. But learning to be on our own and to be able to socialise with other people are both important for mental health and well-being.

Try it yourself

Make some notes on the following, and retain them for future reference. Observe how you change over time.

1. What are my responsibilities as a social being?
2. How does connection with other people affect me?
3. Do I enter into relationships which become exploitive? How do I deal with this tendency?
4. What are the important relationships in my life at the moment?
5. What do I need to change in my life to find more time for others?
6. How can I avoid becoming a doormat when I make myself more available?
7. How can I maintain healthy boundaries?
8. What happens when we do not learn healthy boundaries in our families?

Having fun

Good humour is not expensive. It is free. The playful child in us used to laugh a lot. We can foster laughter and fun again. People often become too serious when they are involved in hard work and struggle to survive financially and emotionally. The funny side of us may be dormant, but it is still there. How much fun have you in your life at this time? When we are anxious and low, we are less likely to look for fun.

When the pressure mounts and the stress levels rise, we are inclined to take everything too seriously. When this happens, we become irritable. Before we realise it, we feel annoyed and upset at small things. When this happens, we can ask ourselves, "Does it really matter?" If it does, then ask the next question: "Will it still matter in two weeks' time?" If it still matters, then we need to get to grips with what needs to be done.

Getting things into perspective is important. If we overreact, irritation increases. This can lead to negativity, feelings of low self-worth and general unhappiness with our work and life. Having fun, by using our sense of humour and seeing the lighter side of life, increases our capacity for happiness. People are attracted to people who enjoy life. Most people enjoy enthusiasm and humour.

Learn to transcend your worries because worries can take the fun out of living. Try to let go of all your thoughts and preoccupations. Put them on hold for a few moments. Live in the present moment. Sit for a moment quietly. Observe your breathing. Observe whatever happens to your body as you inhale and exhale.

What does it mean to have fun? Can we find time for leisure activities? For activities that we enjoy such as gardening, walking, singing, reading novels, or listening to music? Can we become more accepting of self and others? Can we stop worrying what others might think of us? Particularly when things get tough, relaxation is important. Life can be exciting and adventurous every day.

Keeping our home tidy

Do I air my living space regularly? Is there chaos in my rooms? Or perhaps I am too orderly and scrupulous? Keep your bedroom airy, dark and peaceful. Keep your home a healthy place in which to work and relax.

Conclusions

Many things will help us to live a healthy life. Good self-esteem is a central factor. Physical exercise will keep us fit and healthy. Enough – and healthy – food will provide us with the energy which we need. Sufficient liquid will help us to maintain good health. Our posture has an enormous impact on our health. The way we breathe will contribute to our wellbeing. Stillness, silence, prayer and meditation are central for our relationship with God. This relationship is basic to our life. It gives meaning and purpose to our existence. Our intellect will support us when we grow old, provided we exercise it. Without enough sleep we cannot function well. A healthy mind in a healthy body in a healthy house will keep our life healthy.